DESIGN GUIDE FOR SECURE ADULT CORRECTIONAL FACILITIES

American Correctional Association

This publication may be ordered from:

American Correctional Association / 4321 Hartwick Road, Suite L-208 /
College Park, Maryland 20740

This project was supported by Grant #EA-0 awarded by the National Institute of Corrections, United States Department of Justice. Points of view or opinions stated in this publication are those of the American Correctional Association and do not necessarily represent the official position of the United States Department of Justice.

AMERICAN CORRECTIONAL ASSOCIATION

H. G. "GUS" MOELLER
President

ANTHONY P. TRAVISONO
Executive Director

W. HARDY RAUCH
Correctional Consultant
Director, Special Projects

NATIONAL INSTITUTE OF CORRECTIONS

ALLEN F. BREED
Director

WILLIAM K. WILKEY
Chief, Prisons Division

AARON A. BROWN
Project Monitor

RESOURCE AGENCIES

American Institute of
Architects
Washington, D.C.
Michael Cohn, Assistant
Director

Capitol Communication
Systems, Inc.
Crofton, Maryland
Thomas A. Sutty, President

Commission on Accreditation
for Corrections
Rockville, Maryland
Robert Fosen, Executive
Director

Correctional Services of
Canada
Ottawa, Ontario
Donald R. Yeomans,
Commissioner

Federal Correctional
Institution
Memphis, Tennessee
Tony R. Young, Warden

Federal Correctional
Institution
Otisville, New York
Michael Quinlan, Warden

Illinois Department of
Corrections
Springfield, Illinois
Michael P. Lane, Director

Kansas Department of
Corrections
Topeka, Kansas
Donna Bergen, Assistant
Director

Michigan Department of
Corrections
Lansing, Michigan
Perry Johnson, Director

National Institute of
Corrections
Washington, D.C.
Allen Breed, Director

Regional Correctional
Facility at Mercer
Mercer, Pennsylvania
Robert Freeman,
Superintendent

Federal Bureau of Prisons
Washington, D.C.
Norman A. Carlson,
Director

U.S. Medical Center for
Federal Prisoners
Springfield, Missouri
J. S. Petrovsky, Warden

U.S. Penitentiary
Leavenworth, Kansas
Jerry O'Brien, Warden

RESOURCE INDIVIDUALS

John W. Braithwaite
Deputy Commissioner,
Communications
The Correctional Services
of Canada
Ottawa Ontario

Thomas A. Coughlin, III
Commissioner
New York State
Department of
Correctional Services
Albany, New York

Sid Folse, AIA
Henningson, Durham &
Richardson
Dallas, Texas

Roy E. Gerard
Assistant Director, Retired
Federal Bureau of
Prisons
Washington, D.C.

Terrell Don Hutto
President-Elect
American Correctional
Association

Robert Landon
Deputy Director
Virginia Department of
Corrections
Richmond, Virginia

Robert Levinson
Deputy Assistant Director
Federal Bureau of
Prisons
Washington, D.C.

William V. Milliken
Director
Utah Division of
Corrections
Salt Lake City, Utah

Laurel Rans
Entropy Limited
Stillwater, Oklahoma

Francis J. Sheridan, AIA
Director of Planning
New York State
Department of
Corrections
Albany, New York

Maurice H. Sigler
Chairman, Retired
U.S. Parole Commission
Lakeland, Florida

Samuel Sublett, Jr.
Accreditation Manager
Illinois Department
of Corrections
St. Charles, Illinois

CONTENTS

5 ADMINISTRATIVE FUNCTIONS

6 SERVICE FACILITIES

7 SECURITY FEATURES

APPENDIXES

INDEX

Practitioners have long recognized that correctional practices are shaped by the structures in which they are housed. This nation's earliest prison—the Pennsylvania system in the early 1800s and later the Auburn system—were, in fact, designed to carry out what were regarded as appropriate and comprehensive correctional philosophies based on silence, penitence, isolation, and harsh discipline.

As we approach the twenty-first century, correctional philosophy has become more enlightened and more respectful of the complexities of combining secure confinement with opportunities for effective rehabilitation through job training, education, health, and social programs. Yet the so-called fortress prison, sorely outmoded by today's correctional standards and goals, too often remains the most recognizable and best understood model for correctional architecture.

Decisionmakers today must struggle with the question "If not fortresses, what?" This publication, based in large part on successfully operating programs, suggests some practical answers to that question. The guidelines represent a culmination of efforts by the U.S. Department of Justice, through the Federal Bureau of Prisons, the National Institute of Corrections, and the American Correctional Association, to combine the need for secure design with sound management and effective program services.

We present these ideas in the hope that they will encourage decisionmakers to pursue the design and construction of institutions that are safe, humane, efficient, and economical to operate and that will serve the best interests of inmates, staff, and the public at large.

Allen F. Breed, Director
National Institute of Corrections

Readers concerned with the planning and design of correctional institutions are usually interested in two types of books: those that are process-oriented, designed to explore the most advanced procedures for sound planning and those that deal more with specific content, conveying a particular body of knowledge about what should or could be included in the design of a modern institution. This book is of the latter type. It attempts to set forth design concepts based on state-of-the-art correctional programs and operations that have flowered in the 1970s and early 1980s.

During the past decade, a virtual revolution has occurred in many correctional systems transforming the way we are now able to deal with people sentenced to a period of confinement.

The basic foundations for corrections remain the same: the protection of society by incapacitating certain offenders; retribution for the criminal acts of individuals or groups; and deterrence of others who also might be inclined toward criminal activity. Outside of the limited use of capital punishment, the correctional institution still represents the ultimate sanction imposed by a modern society on its members who cannot or will not abide by an accepted code of conduct. What has changed perceptibly is the internal climate, life, and administration of a growing number of institutions. The new attitudes and policies characteristic of these facilities have been forged by forward-looking administrators, many of whose efforts have received encouragement and support from private citizens, public officials, and legislators. While not always understood or appreciated, many court decisions have also assisted correctional managers by mandating greater professionalism and accountability and by calling the public's attention to the necessity for more resources to carry out growing responsibilities.

What are the main elements that distinguish these contemporary practices from the traditional? Greater concern for the safety of both inmates and staff, more humane conditions of confinement, smaller institutions, due process concerning inmate complaints of alleged injustices, broadened public involvement in daily institutional affairs and programs, the location of new facilities closer to major cities to facilitate visiting and strengthen family ties, better training for staff, and more formalized policies and procedures are just some of the important elements characteristic of recent correctional planning.

Some systems have gone even further. This book is based largely on those advanced practices that encourage greater interaction between staff and inmates, the use of decentralized forms of inmate management, reduction of physical barriers separating staff and inmates, and greater reliance on professional supervision of inmates rather than mere observation or policies and procedures that are essentially reactive. The resulting environments, coupled with sound programs, are more normal and offer inmates greater encouragement to take advantage of their period of confinement for self-improvement through bettering their social or work skills, or academic education, or all of these. To the extent that inmates desire to change their behavior as a result of these advanced practices, the criminal justice system will be more effective and the public will be better served.

Gary Mote AIA, Chairman,
ACA Committee for the Design Guide for Secure Adult Correctional Facilities

Anthony P. Travisono, Executive Director,
American Correctional Association

ACKNOWLEDGMENTS

The American Correctional Association, including the Design Guidelines Project Committee, is grateful to the National Institute of Corrections not only for its financial assistance but also for the continued support, encouragement, and helpful advice of its staff throughout this extremely important project. The guidelines contained in this book are also made possible because of the strong support of the Director of the Federal Bureau of Prisons, Norman A. Carlson, and his staff, particularly those in the Bureau's Division of Planning and Development under the direction of Assistant Director Wade Houk. We are especially indebted to Don Voth, Architect, and Deborah Lemonias, Management Analyst, whose yeoman efforts were essential to our success. The primary responsibility for organizing and drafting this document rested on their able shoulders, for which their only compensations are the satisfaction of a job well done and our heartfelt thanks.

In addition, we appreciate the contribution of Sid Folse, AIA, and Scott Winchester, who are with HDR's Criminal Justice Design Center. The architectural diagrams that accompany many of the program sections were prepared by them and donated for use in this publication. These diagrams are valuable tools that help bridge the gap between general program goals and architectural concepts.

The Association is grateful to Gary Mote, AIA, who served as chairman of the group. Throughout the entire process of conceptualization, development, and publication of this material Mr. Mote has been steadfast in establishing high goal expectations to ensure the production of information that is informative, inspirational, and easily translated into practical application.

W. Hardy Rauch
Project Manager

INTRODUCTION

The 1970s was a decade of dynamic change in the development of correctional facility design. Correctional philosophy had changed dramatically during the 1960s. New programs were being implemented, tested, and modified, with facility design evolving to respond to the new trends. These changes, in conjunction with overcrowding, major riots, antiquated facilites, court interventions, public outcries, legislative changes of sentencing statutes, philosophical shifts from the "Medical Model" to a "Justice Model," and changes in or abolition of parole, had a dramatic effect on prison design and construction. The purpose of this book is to convey the results of that process of fermentation that occurred in correctional institution design during the past decade. It is hoped that this text will be a useful guide to correctional systems embarking on new facility construction in the future, as they attempt to meet the ever growing demands of the changes taking place about them.

The design guidelines contained in this book are based on a specific philosophical foundation:

- Offenders are sentenced to confinement as punishment for a criminal offense, but not for further punishment in the hands of their keepers or by inordinately harsh conditions in their physical environments.
- Inmates can expect to be confined humanely and safely.
- Staff can expect to carry out their responsibilities professionally in a safe environment.
- The institutional atmosphere should be as normal as possible for the welfare of both inmates and staff and, ultimately, for that of the public, as conditions during confinement will likely influence behavior after release.
- During confinement, inmates should be provided with opportunities for, and encouraged to participate in, institutional programs for self-improvement in areas such as academic, vocational, and social skills.
- Staff should interact directly with inmates. They should not be separated by architectural barriers that communicate a negative attitude by management or that impede the open, interpersonal communications necessary for a positive climate in any human culture.
- A reasonable balance should be struck between the security features of a secure correctional facility and an architectural environment that projects a spirit of openness and reconciliation.

This guide does not begin with the earliest steps of sound planning for a new correctional facility. Good facility planning should follow from a dynamic process of ongoing evaluation of a correctional system's requirements, a process that includes careful coordination of planned activities among all elements of the criminal justice system. This process requires a mechanism whereby an advisory or policy planning group conducts periodic analyses of the significant factors affecting the total system and formulates broad policy for component organizations. While the planning group can be composed of either independent, public-spirited citizens or public officials working within the criminal justice system, it is best to have both groups represented. Strong representation by public officials active in day-to-day management will usually expedite the implementation of new policy because the success or failure of new directions ultimately depends on the support and leadership of these managers.

In formulating policy, the following matters should receive periodic review:

- Crime, arrest, and incarceration rates
- Impact of pending legislative changes
- Inmate demographics
- Shifts in civilian population
- Sentencing policy
- Parole policy
- Public attitudes
- System resources
- Alternatives to confinement, including

    fines

    restitution programs

    probation

    other community corrections programs such as work release centers
- Relationships to non-correctional-system programs, such as

    health

    mental health

    academic education

    vocational education

    drug abuse

- Adequacy of the existing system, including facilities.

The importance of good systems planning cannot be overemphasized. Not only are new institutions expensive to construct; the cost of maintaining and operating them for, say 50 years, may exceed capital costs by 20 to 25 times. These lifetime costs are so significant that every effort should be made to strike a proper balance between community and non-community programs, as the former are generally less costly and often more suitable for many offenders if placement is based on an objective classification system.

But sound systems planning and the appropriate use of alternatives to confinement, while necessary, will not in themselves preclude the need for new correctional facilities. New correctional institutions are clearly needed to house the growing populations being committed by the courts to already crowded and often antiquated prisons. It is at this point in the correctional planning process that the guidelines expressed in this book become relevant.

To confine the scope of this book to a range with the most practical and

Inmates can expect to be confined safely and humanely and to interact directly with staff.

widespread application, its focus is on that spectrum of correctional facility design where the largest amount of construction activity is expected to take place—medium security institutions with a capacity for up to 500 inmates.

Most authorities agree that maximum security institutions are required for no more than 5 percent to 15 percent of a correctional system's population, and many systems currently have sufficient capacity for this group. For the purposes of this text, maximum security inmates are defined as those with a history of extreme violence or behavior, or whose behavior during confinement seriously threatens the safety of other inmates as well as staff, or whose risk of escape would pose a significant threat to the community.

About one-third of a correctional system's population can be placed in minimum security facilities. Such facilities are much less expensive to construct and operate than secure institutions, and they usually require no perimeter fence other than a general-purpose fence to discourage non-authorized traffic in or about the main compound. Surplus military buildings, schools, hospitals, and mental health facilities can often be adapted for this segment of the inmate population.

Between the two categories of maximum and minimum security institutions lies the wide range generally referred to as medium security facilities. While specific security construction will vary at the extremes within this range, general construction features remain reasonably constant. For example, at a lower-level medium security facility, the general features of a compound fence such as location, size, and spacing are about the same as those required for a higher-level medium security (close security) institution. The distinctions among medium security facilities have more to do with such features as the relative use and sophistication of intrusion alarm systems, barrier wire, and mobile vehicular patrols.

The guidelines presented in this book can be applied to institutions housing males, females, or both in a co-correctional setting. Institutions designed by these guidelines have housed males at one point, females at another, and both in co-correctional programs. Because the spaces within

Campus plans (opposite), which provide outdoor, open circulation and dispersed housing, offer greater diversity, provide exercise, and stimulate the senses. This in turn reduces the tensions inherent in traditional enclosed corridor plans. (Left) Good design and careful placement of core facilities and housing units can facilitate interaction between staff and inmates and foster a positive atmosphere within the institution.

the facility are adaptable for a variety of activities, most differences between a male facility and a female facility can be addressed through programmatic or operational changes. Planners should be alert, however, to any differences detailed in this book that could affect the facility design. For example, female inmates generally require more medical services than males do, and this may have a slight impact on the design of the medical facility, such as the number of patient beds. Whether the institution houses males, females, or both, however, the overall space requirements and division of spaces discussed in this book remain virtually the same for all groups.

Indeed, one of the substantial benefits of following this guide is the strong adaptability of the resulting facilities. In corrections, as in many other fields, change is constant. A perpetual ebb and flow of changing population characteristics will occur during the life of any facility, and physical plants must be highly adaptable to meet the varying requirements. Facilities designed by these guidelines not only will easily accommodate both male and female in-mates, but also can serve populations of varying ages with very diverse profiles and differing security classification levels and program needs. As a rule, the physical modifications needed to accommodate such population shifts will be relatively minor, if any.

Another feature of these institutions is their economy of contruction and operating expense. Direct comparisons between traditional and more contemporary facilities are difficult to make, and differing management styles and philosophies often will produce significantly different architectural responses. Broad measures can be applied, however, that suggest that the contemporary facilities generated by these guidelines are certainly no more expensive to construct and operate and in fact can be less costly. The reliance on excessive hardware and extensive secure construction in most traditional facilities is a costly burden to bear in a climate of scarce resources.

Staff Issues

Staffing has a direct impact on the design of a facility. The greater the number of staff anticipated in a functional area, the more space needed to accommodate that staff. If, for example, some business office functions such as procurement are handled centrally at headquarters or in regional offices, a smaller financial staff, with concomitantly less space, is required at the institution. The employment of males in female institutions, or vice versa, requires certain provisions for privacy. In addition, designers should consider the features needed to make recruitment and employment of the handicapped a realistic goal.

Inmate population projections provide information about the racial and cultural makeup of those who will be committed to an institution. One staffing goal should be to recruit and select employees who will adequately represent these racial and cultural backgrounds, thereby decreasing the risks of inmates' misinterpretation of rules or confrontations based on real or imagined differences.

Not only does staffing affect the facility design, but, more subtly, the design of the facility affects the number and type of staff required to operate it effectively. This is especially true with security posts. Throughout

To confine the scope of this book to a range with the most practical and widespread application, its focus is on that spectrum of correctional facility design where the largest amount of construction activity is expected to take place—medium security institutions with a capacity for up to 500 inmates.

the design phases, careful attention must be paid to any staff requirements "built in" to the facility design. For example, the configuration of buildings on the site can create numerous hiding places that may inordinately increase the potential for escape or other security problems; such areas require more intensive surveillance, which increases the number of staff needed to supervise the institution effectively. Another example of the impact of design on staffing is the desire of some administrators to construct a sally port used only for the entrance and exit of inmates. A sally port (discussed in detail in the section on Entrances) requires considerable staff time to operate. A sally port for inmates would create an additional and perhaps unnecessary break in the perimeter security that would require additional staff time to supervise. Experience has shown that inmates can be safely admitted and discharged through the institution's main entrance sally port, eliminating the need for a separate inmate entrance and the associated demands on staff. In addition, the vehicular service sally port can be used in an emergency.

During the pre-planning stages it is important to determine the number of staff required for each functional area at the facility and to analyze the impact of each design decision on staffing requirements. It is difficult to develop a methodology for objectively determining specific personnel requirements. Correctional standards, for example, express personnel needs in terms of ultimate goals such as 24-hour coverage. References in the text to typical staffing patterns in individual programs should be considered as general statements only. Each correctional system has to design its institutional programs and allocate staff according to its own specific mission, philosophy, and physical plant characteristics.

Staffing levels should be reasonably well defined before embarking on architectural design. The facility discussed in this book is based on a set of staffing guidelines, developed by federal correctional program managers, that specifies the number and type of staff required to operate a particular program. These comprehensive staffing guidelines, developed for facilities of all security levels, are consistent with the mainstream philosophy woven throughout this guide and may be helpful as a reference point from which correctional agencies can determine their unique staffing needs. A good case can be made for additional staff depending on the specific type of population to be housed, and a number of systems operate at higher levels. A further discussion of how the staffing guidelines were developed and a list of the guidelines themselves are contained in Appendix 1.

Standards

Throughout the preparation of this book, full consideration was given to the standards developed by the American Correctional Association (ACA) in cooperation with the Commission on Accreditation for Corrections and those developed by the U.S. Department of Justice. The designers of new institutions are urged to become thoroughly familiar with current editions of both of these standards. Appendix 2 contains many of the standards affecting physical plant design, taken from *Standards for Adult Correctional Institutions, Second Edition,* published by the American Correctional Association.

Emergency Facilities

There are times when over-crowding reaches such high levels that correctional administrators must undertake emergency measures to address the problem. The courts have also frequently directed that certain remedies be employed to relieve the effects of overcrowding as quickly as possible. In extreme cases, tents or mobile trailers have been used for emergency housing. Some coastal states have even considered the temporary use of ocean-going ships, permanently anchored in a harbor. Such makeshift structures should be viewed only as temporary remedies. Security, staffing, sanitation, and health considerations often make these interventions undesirable.

An approach that has gained popularity in recent years is the use of prefabricated modular units, or manufactured component systems. Depending on the capabilities of manufacturers and market conditions, conventional prefabricated modular units such as those used for classrooms or housing can quickly provide program space or minimum security housing. These conventional units are usually constructed of wood or thin metal and therefore are not adaptable for spaces requiring secure construction. Institutions housing inmates at higher levels of security can use prefabricated modular units made of concrete or steel plates. These units are available from several manufacturers, and the components can be delivered to the construction site and assembled into a permanent facility in less time than that required for conventional construction.

Experience indicates that the use of permanent modular facilities can save 5 percent to 10 percent of the construction time needed for more conventional construction using the phased, or fast-track, scheduling process. The evidence is less clear as to whether the permanent, secure modular systems actually produce any dollar savings over the long term. A cost-benefit analysis of modular facilities versus more conventional construction that considers the life cycle cost, staffing implications, and quality of the resulting environments may indicate that total "costs" for the modular facilities are higher.

Overcrowding, a problem confronting many correctional agencies, has been addressed in some places with prefabricated or modular units (left). Generally, such structures should be viewed only as temporary remedies. The use of secure glazing materials in contemporary correctional designs creates an atmosphere of openness (opposite).

1
PLANNING, DESIGN, CONSTRUCTION PROCESS AND ISSUES

PRE-DESIGN PLANNING

Pre-design planning refers to certain activities, discussed below, that are the primary responsibility of the correctional agency. It concerns planning for a specific facility that has already been deemed necessary by the agency and, perhaps, already authorized by the legislature as a result of prior systems master planning. Pre-design planning is a specialty and should not be relegated to the architect, although some of it is often done with the help of an architect. If the agency does not have adequate staff or expertise in this area, one of the sizeable number of individuals or firms that specialize in pre-design planning should be retained to assist the agency.

What are the important steps in the process?

The agency first should form a steering committee to oversee the project throughout the entire planning and design process. This committee should be composed of the agency officials who will have primary responsibility for facility operations and inmate programs once the facility is constructed. Membership should also include representatives from other elements of the criminal justice system, such as the judiciary, the legislature, and community corrections. One committee member, usually the chairman, should be designated as principal liaison between the agency and the design professionals. This person should be part of the agency's upper management team to ensure that the overall direction of the project, as well as the specific purpose of the proposed facility, is consistent with management's general philosophy. Such a person is in a position to sense the relative importance and intricacies of certain issues, and has immediate access to other members of upper management so that problems or questions can be resolved quickly. The importance of timely decisions cannot be overemphasized. Without them, a project will flounder, designers will be frustrated, efficiency will be sacrificed, and costs will grow in proportion to the resulting confusion and delay.

The initial tasks for the steering committee should be as follows:

- Define the specific mission of the institution, including how it relates to the rest of the correctional system.
- Articulate a philosophy for operating the institution. What are the specific program goals? What kind of social and interpersonal climate is desired between inmates? between staff and inmates?
- Establish the capacity of the institution.
- Gather information on the projected inmate population for the purpose of institutional programming. This information includes profiles on age, sex, race, prior and

The importance of timely decisions cannot be overemphasized. Without them, a project will flounder, designers will be frustrated, efficiency will be sacrificed, and costs will grow in proportion to the resulting confusion and delay.

current offenses, length of sentences and estimated length of sentences to be served, socioeconomic data, residency, drug and alcohol abuse, mental and medical health status, educational background, religious affiliation, vocational training, and work history. An objective classification system can be extremely helpful in this area.

- Gather information on existing "model" institutions; assess problems in existing institutions; assess the availability of community resources for institutional programs and identify potential programming options.
- Determine the security needs of the projected population.
- Estimate the number of staff required by functional area.
- Define the general type of physical environment desired to complement the planned inmate program and efforts of staff.
- Establish a preliminary budget for all stages of facility development: planning, design, construction, purchase of equipment, facility activation, and staffing.

The owner agency should form a steering committee to oversee the project. The committee should be composed of agency officials who will have primary responsibility for operations and programs once the facility is constructed, as well as representatives from other elements of the criminal justice system such as the judiciary, the legislature, and community corrections.

- Develop a mechanism and time table to prepare for activation of the facility. Activation planning should begin early in the process even though activation activities will not intensify until the months just before completion of construction. Many new institutions fail to realize in full the rich potential inherent in any newly constructed facility because of inadequate attention to activation planning and staff development activities. Countless examples exist of facilities that cost millions of dollars to design and construct and yet deteriorated rapidly after opening because of poor activation planning.

While some of these issues can be addressed only tentatively at the pre-design stage, this early planning is crucial to the basic development of the design. As planning and design proceeds, early tenets will be continuously tested and adjusted and the design fine-tuned as new information becomes available.

Consulting experts in other agencies can be very helpful in developing the institution's services and programs, such as health and education. The contributions of non-correctional agency representatives frequently translate into improved services, lower operational and capital costs.

Many correctional agencies rely on other government agencies with statutory authority for constructing government structures, such as public works departments, to contract for design and construction services. The staff of such non-correctional agencies are rarely well versed in correctional philosophy and programs

or the features peculiar to correctional facilities. Yet they will bear the responsibility for delivering a successful facility within budget. Such an arrangement inherently creates opportunity for conflict and misunderstanding unless the steering committee carefully structures the relationship between the user-agency, the "contracting agency," and all those who provide contract services. Either the steering committee or the head of the user-agency should designate one person with final authority as the point-of-contact with the contracting agency. This person, usually called the project manager, serves as a "right hand" to the steering committee chairman. While there should be open communication between others representing various interests, the user-

agency's project manager and the contracting agency's representative must have authority to make timely decisions for both agencies.

One of the most important roles of the steering committee chariman is to establish clear lines of responsibility and authority. Organization efficiency depends on well-defined relationships between all participants. Clear role definition is especially critical when the design professionals enter the process. Too frequently, designers find themselves with too many "bosses," a situation that produces costly delays and changes, frayed emotions, expensive facilities, and poor. design solutions.

The purpose of this text is not to provide detailed guidance on the pre-design phase of the planning process, but rather to emphasize its impor-

tance. For additional information, agencies should feel free to call on any of the following organizations, some of whom are equipped to provide excellent technical assistance on particular agency needs.

American Correctional Association
4321 Hartwick Road, Suite L-208
College Park, Maryland 20740

American Institute of Architects
1735 New York Avenue, N.W.
Washington, D.C. 20006

Commission on Accreditation
for Corrections
6110 Executive Boulevard, Suite 600
Rockville, Maryland 20852

National Institute of Corrections
(NIC)
320 First Street, N.W.
Washington, D.C. 20534

National Institute of Corrections
Jail Center
1790 30th Street, Suite 140
Boulder, Colorado 80301

National Institute of Corrections
National Information Center
1790 30th Street, Suite 130
Boulder, Colorado 80301

State Clearinghouses for Criminal
Justice Planning and Architecture

Organizational efficiency depends on well-defined relationships between all participants. Too frequently, designers find themselves with too many "bosses," a situation that produces costly delays and changes, frayed emotions, expensive facilities, and poor design solutions.

Correctional facilities should be located as close as possible to major metropolitan areas. It is also desirable for the location to be near the home community from which the largest number of inmates will come.

Metropolitan locations are generally easily accessible, enabling relatives of inmates to visit more frequently. This is significant because maintenance of family ties is an important factor in inmates' adjustment to their communities after a period of confinement. Locations in or near major communities also aid in recruiting personnel, especially highly trained professional staff, as well as staff who represent the racial and cultural backgrounds of the inmate population. Part-time professional specialists and program services are more readily available in these locations, making possible such options as contract academic or vocational training programs and medical services.

Locations near major cities also provide a variety of housing options for staff. Educational facilities for the children of staff are often better than

SITE SELECTION AND ACQUISITION

those in more remote areas, and there are more opportunities for staff to extend their formal education by attending community colleges or universities. Shopping, recreation, and entertainment facilities are more abundant. All of these factors not only make staff recruitment easier, they also play an important role in maintaining good staff morale and in reducing turnover among trained personnel.

While the size of a site may vary widely, as a general rule a facility for up to 500 inmates should be located on a site of 150 acres. Although some modern facilities are located on

smaller parcels, a 150-acre site offers flexibility in planning the institution's compound, parking, roads, and security perimeter. It also affords adequate "buffer" zones around the institution. If a farm program is planned, the necessary land must be added to the acreage recommended.

Ideally, the site topography should be relatively flat with good drainage or gently rolling; otherwise, considerable expense can be incurred for grading the site. Since few sites meet all ideal criteria, trade-offs must often be considered, such as accepting a site with hilly or rougher terrain than desired. Many good building sites have been developed from less-than-desirable terrain at reasonable costs, and it is no longer considered necessary to flatten the site of a correctional institution in order to obtain good security features. Observation sight lines can often be enhanced with irregular terrain as long as consideration is given to the arrangement of buildings and proper security features. Irregular terrain can also be more attractive than flat landscapes and can help relieve the boredom associated with many types of correctional architecture.

Good access roads to the site are essential to avoid costly road development. Appropriate utility systems should also be available or expandable by the local utility company to minimize both initial capital expenditures and lifetime operating expenses for the institution.

It may be advantageous to locate a new institution adjacent or close to other government facilities, especially law enforcement or existing correctional facilities. The nearby communities will be familiar with such programs and may have few, if any, concerns about the proposed institution. Occasionally such land is already owned by the government entity involved and the site acquisition process will be easier and the costs lower.

Most communities have planning agencies whose role is to help determine local growth and land-use policy. Working with administrative authorities and public works departments, the planning agencies attempt to implement policy established by the community leadership by regulat-

An artist's conception of a facility superimposed on an aerial photograph can help planners and the public visualize a proposed facility on a particular site.

ing zoning, utility development, road development, and building codes. The correctional authority should try to coordinate correctional planning with local planning agencies to ensure that potential sites will be serviced by all necessary utilities and roads, and will conform to established planning policy. Local planning agencies can be a valuable source of useful information for selecting sites. Land-use, topography, utility, zoning, demographic, and public transportation maps, along with aerial photographs, are very helpful for identifying and evaluating any available undeveloped sites. Other useful sources of information include local real estate firms, the classified sections of local newspapers, and the local tax assessor's office.

Zoning codes usually do not address correctional facilities, nor do communities explicitly provide a zoned area for their development. Because the location of correctional facilities is often controversial and so few are built in comparison with other community facilities, zoning boards simply do not include plans for them. Federal and state govern-

ment agencies, however, are not required to comply with local zoning plans. The concept of eminent domain provides statutory authority for governments to exercise ultimate jurisdiction over land-use policy if it is determined that such actions are for the public good. But it is recommended that this power not be exercised whenever there is significant community opposition. It is normally better to work with the community leadership and the zoning authorities to obtain a permit for land acquisition. If the proper political and community climate is developed, obtaining a special permit is seldom a problem, and the harmonious relationship established with the community will pay dividends in the future. Cases exist where the friendly exercise of eminent domain has facilitated acquisition of a site once community support has been established.

Another important issue in site selection concerns environmental protection policy. Many states have enacted laws that require an assessment of the environmental impact of proposed projects. In addition, the National Environmental Policy Act of 1969 may be a consideration if fed-

eral funds are involved in the project. This act prevents significant expenditures of federal funds without adequate assessment of potential environmental impacts; states that have enacted environmental policy laws have similar requirements.

Answering the following questions will help determine if environmental problems exist for sites under consideration.

Will the implementation of a proposed correctional facility or program:

- Lead to a significant increase in air, water, or soil pollution, or soil erosion?
- Lead to poor land-use?
- Destroy or derogate an important recreational area?
- Substantially alter the behavior pattern of wildlife or interfere with important breeding, nesting, or feeding grounds?
- Disturb the ecological balance of land or water areas?
- Have an adverse impact on areas of historical, cultural, educational, or scientific significance?
- Have an adverse aesthetic or visual effect?
- Lead to a substantial adverse

Communities adjacent to proposed correctional institutions will often object, some strenuously. Their primary concerns are personal safety and the potential impact of the facility on property values. These are understandable fears that should be recognized and addressed.

change in the character of the community?

During the site acquisition stage, these issues can be addressed more fully in a formal report. Information on the National Environmental Policy Act of 1969 and environmental assessments can be obtained from the Council on Environmental Quality and the U.S. Environmental Protection Agency. Local environmental standards and regulations may be obtained from state health, conservation, and environmental agencies. Additional information is usually available through local and state historical societies, public interest groups, and state and national geological survey agencies.

Timely selection and acquisition of the site is important. The site should be selected as soon as possible after the project is approved, and certainly before the design development phase commences. The architectural and engineering team should be engaged prior to selection of the site so that it can help assess the relative merits of alternative locations. While an agency may believe it is necessary, for timesaving or political reasons, to proceed with the facility design prior to site selection, this approach frequently leads to certain sacrifices and added costs.

Communities adjacent to proposed correctional institutions will often object, some strenuously. Their primary concerns are personal safety and the potential impact of the facility on property values. These are legitimate fears that should be recognized and addressed. Fortunately, both are usually unfounded. When inmates escape from institutions, for example, the last thing they want is to call attention to their escape; they simply want to get away from the area as quickly as possible. Numerous examples of fast-rising property values in the vicinity of correctional institutions put to rest the myth of destroyed property values. For instance, a recent study in Wisconsin found that a facility built in the Green Bay area had no impact on property values when compared to other sections of the metropolitan area. In fact, whenever an agency announces its intention to close an existing correctional facility, there usually is broad public opposition.

Presenting these facts to communities can shift public opinion, if not in favor, at least to a neutral position about the location of the proposed facility. Meeting with key people and groups in the community to explain the proposed program can alleviate concerns before they become magnified. Knowledge of local power structures is important when proposing a new facility in a community. Judges, sheriffs, business and community leaders, and elected officials are often the individuals who determine whether an institution is welcomed or not. It also is important to point out to communities the economic advantages of new correctional institutions, including the stable employment opportunities they represent. For this reason alone, many communities openly solicit the nearby location of an institution, and some will even furnish a site at no charge.

ARCHITECTURAL PROGRAM

Almost all complex design projects need a transitional or conceptual bridge between the general mission and operational objectives of a proposed facility and the physical design solution. The purpose of the architectural program is to supply that bridge, and the process of preparing the program is a crucial phase in converting goals into ideas that will in turn produce complementary architectural solutions.

Development of the architectural program is the next stage in the planning process following pre-design planning. Indeed, the program evolves from an analysis of the issues that surfaced during that earlier stage, including the different kinds of programs and services to be provided, their mission within the facility, the number of staff by functional area, and the relationships between and within departments.

The architectural program serves as a written guide or set of instructions to the designer. It should be both concise and specific, and should identify the following:

- General design approach, including mission and characteristics of the facility

- All physical space requirements, including the square feet needed for each space and its attendant functional description
- Relative locations or adjacencies between spaces
- Staff positions and adjacencies
- Special equipment needs.

Both the project budget and schedule should be updated at this stage. It is also desirable to identify the correctional standards that will affect the facility's design.

Typically, the user-agency is responsible for preparing the architectural program. If the steering committee or project manager lacks the necessary expertise, an architectural team or other specialists in this field can be retained to produce the program. Even if the agency is well versed in this procedure, the use of contract specialists at this early stage can produce fresh ideas and approaches. In fact, development of the architectural program, especially its review, is best done in an open forum involving a multidisciplinary group of correctional managers and designers, freely exchanging ideas about how best to provide services and exploring the issues and constraints of a correctional environment. The programming team, along with agency representatives, should also visit existing facilities and talk with inmates as well as staff to generate ideas, determine what designs have worked well in practice, and learn about potential design improvements.

This period is the most fluid stage of design. Even though conflicting goals or ideas from earlier planning will always emerge, it is relatively easy to make corrections at this stage with little expense in time or money. Indeed, this is a period for testing earlier assumptions. Not only is it crucial to good planning that the agency steering committee heavily involve itself in this phase, it also can be a rewarding experience for everyone.

The purpose of the architectural program is to supply that bridge between the general mission of a proposed facility and the physical design solution. The process of preparing the program is a crucial phase in converting goals into ideas that will in turn produce complementary architectural solutions.

Selecting the Architectural and Engineering Team

Of the many decisions to be made during the planning process, selection of the architect is one of the most important. The architect and the design team should possess both technical and managerial skills. Equally significant, but often inadequately considered, is the issue of good communication between the design team and the "owner." or client. Agencies should ensure that the architect will not only engage in strong dialogue, but will also structure a broad range of meetings and tours of existing facilities to gain insight into the project's unique requirements. Such insights often concern subtleties of tone and style that cannot be reflected in formal written programs or narrative documents, yet which have a powerful influence on the future physical environment of the facility and the climate created for effective program management.

There are several ways to approach the selection of an architect. The three methods generally followed are comparative selection, direct selection, and design com-

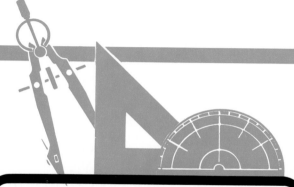

ARCHITECTURAL AND ENGINEERING SERVICES

petitions. Some agencies also hire a construction manager who helps in the selection (see "Construction Management Method" later in this chapter).

Most architectural commissions are awarded by either comparative or direct selection. In either case, it is suggested that a local architect be retained. A local firm is of great help concerning local codes and conditions that may be unique to the area. If local architects are not well versed in correctional architecture, then a local architect should be retained in association with a firm or consultant that specializes in this field.

Regardless of the method used, the architect chosen should be some-

one with whom there can be a relationship of absolute confidence and trust. The architect should be thoroughly familiar with established building techniques and various standards, including ACA standards for correctional facilities. Once the decision to award the commission has been made, the owner and architect should conclude their negotiations with a written agreement so that all matters between them are clearly understood. Proceeding with the knowledge that a capable architect has been selected, the agency should be assured of a pleasurable and rewarding experience throughout the design process.

Comparative Selection

Comparative selection is the method most commonly used for selecting an architect, whether the selection is made by an individual or by a group. The selection process typically follows five basic steps:

1. The agency issues a formal or informal request for proposals (RFP), identifying the nature of the project, the budget, and the dominant factors to be considered in the selection pro-

A mid-point in the schematic design phase—following acceptance of the "bubble" drawings and the "concepts"—is the preparation of dimensional floor plans. These drawings indicate floor areas, space relationships, adjacencies, and methods of entry and exit from rooms and buildings.

cess. Selection factors usually include the firm's experience with similar projects, its proximity to the project, its technical qualifications, and the size of its available work force. Interested firms submit their qualifications and ask to be considered for the work.

2. The proposals are reviewed and a "short list" of several firms, usually three to five, are selected for further consideration.

3. Usually the agency interviews each firm on the "short list." A personal interview gives the agency or its representative an opportunity to find out more about the architect's attitudes, philosophy, and personality. All major staff who will be assigned to the project should attend the interview. It is also important to determine who will provide any consulting services needed for various elements such as the mechanical, electrical, structural, or security systems. Enough time should be allowed to permit the applicant to make a thorough presentation; forty-five minutes to one and one-half hours is normally adequate.

4. Sometimes the agency investigates the architect's former clients and projects to determine levels of client satisfaction and to gain insight into the architect's ability and ingenuity in solving design problems. The agency should keep in mind, however, that previous projects may have been substantially limited or restricted by the client's architectural program or budget.

5. Following the interviews and investigations, firms should be ranked in order of preference and notified of the decision within a few days. The architectural fee should not be a consideration in this ranking; final negotiations should be conducted with the best-qualified firm. The negotiations should be thorough and complete so that both the owner and the architect understand the expected services and the associated costs, including the amount of the fee. The user-agency's obligations should also be clearly defined. Items to be considered include expenses— for example, travel, per diem, printing costs—and services to be performed by others, such as surveys, soil borings, and other investigations. Agreement should also be reached on any other requirements that may affect the cost of professional services, such as special programming or evaluation services; services during construction, such as full-time, on-site construction observation; preparation of "as-built," or record, drawings; and the selection of equipment and furnishings.

If the negotiations with the highest-ranking firm are unsuccessful, negotiations are held with the next firm, but never with more than one firm simultaneously.

Direct Selection

The direct selection method allows an agency to select an architect with relative ease and little expense. The selection is made on the basis of reputation, personal acquaintance, and recommendations of former clients. All criteria addressed in the comparative selection procedure should be considered.

Design Competitions

The competition method of selection provides agencies with a way to compare various design solutions for a particular project. A competition also gives people skilled in special aspects of architecture an opportunity to exercise their creativity, and it enables talented architects to gain recognition.

Because a competition is more expensive and time consuming than other selection methods, its use has been limited, for the most part, to large civic projects. But the method should not be rejected out of hand. Advancing the state of the art can, on occasion, be worth the extra time and expense.

Since verbal communication is limited in a competition, the agency must prepare a well-thought-out and comprehensive architectural program. This is important to the agency as well as the competitors, for it ensures that the resulting designs are relevant to the agency's needs.

Participation in design competitions is expensive for firms. Adequate compensation should be provided for the winner and the top three to five runners-up. Competitions dealing with highly specialized facilities frequently limit competitors to a few selected firms, all of whom receive compensation.

Selection by this method requires compliance with rules that will result in a fair competition and establish equitable relations between the owner and all competitors. For these reasons, the Code for Architectural Competitions, published by the American Institute of Architects (AIA), should be followed explicitly.

Responsibilities of the Architectural and Engineering Team

Most architectural and engineering (A/E) teams can provide a wide array of services for the design and construction of a facility. Over the years, some of these services have become part of what is now called a "basic services" contract, which includes the following elements:

- Probable construction costs, analyses, and controls
- Schematic design
- Design development
- Preparation of construction contract documents
- Assistance in construction bidding
- Observation of the construction activity

In addition to requiring some or all of the basic services, the agency may want the design team to assist with the following "additional services":

- Site selection
- Preparation of the architectural program
- Security systems design
- Landscape design
- Interior design (including furnishings)
- Graphic design
- Presentation materials, models, and mock-ups (valuable for laymen to understand the project)
- Record drawings
- Design of off-site utilities
- Environmental reports
- Life-cycle cost analysis
- Staffing analysis
- Funding alternatives
- Detailed cost estimating
- Public information assistance.

The typical A/E contract for nongovernment work includes all of the items listed as basic services. The typical contract for government agencies will probably exclude preparation of certain bidding documents, known as the "boiler plate," and may exclude assistance in the bidding process and observation of the construction work as well. At the same time, additional services may be added. The agency must decide which services it requires and negotiate with the A/E firm accordingly.

As the general plan assumes a more understandable form, many people begin to relate to the project more easily than they could at earlier stages. Agency personnel often do not seriously engage in earlier design activities because of their unfamiliarity with the processes. Nonetheless, it is very important for them to be involved in each stage and to exercise their approval authority with full knowledge of the implications.

One of the most important decisions to be made during the planning process is the selection of the architect. In addition to technical and managerial skills, an essential criteria in selecting a candidate is good communication skills. Only through continuing, open dialogue between the architect and other members of the planning team can a successful project be insured.

Cost Estimating

The importance of accurate cost estimates for the proposed project cannot be overemphasized. Estimates must encompass all segments of the project, including, but not limited to, site preparation, utility systems, and construction of buildings. It is crucial that these estimates be reviewed and analyzed during each phase of the design process to ensure that the design remains within the budget.

Many architectural firms rely on their own staff to estimate costs, and many are quite successful at accurately predicting these costs. Nevertheless, a good case can be made for the use of an independent cost estimator who is psychologically more distant from the design and thus not burdened with the mixed emotions that can emerge around trade-offs between the budget and better materials or more attractive features. The use of a well-qualified independent estimator can provide confidence to both the owner and the architect that the project will likely be within the budget.

Schematic Design Phase

Using the architectural program and the knowledge gained from conferences with agency personnel, the design team begins the schematic phase by diagramming the spaces required in the facility and their relationships, or adjacencies, to one another. Often these diagrams are in the form of "bubbles." Some diagrams show relationships between major functions—for example, the relationships between housing units,

educational programs, and dining and food preparation areas. Others are more detailed and show all the spaces included in a particular building or functional area, such as all of the individual spaces in the education department. Circulation patterns for each area are also indicated. When the diagrams are complete, the agency reviews them for approval before the designers proceed to the next stage.

The next stage of schematic design is sometimes called "concepts." Concept drawings illustrate the broad outlines of the project and show how planned buildings and improvements such as fences and roads will relate to the site and any features peculiar to the site, including zoning or set-back regulations. Major pedestrian and vehicular circulation patterns are delineated, special utility features are identified, and—for the first time in the design process—the drawings begin to reflect actual dimensions.

In some projects, designers will begin to study the three-dimensional relationships of structures ("massing"), which involves working with vertical elevations as well as floor plans. This process helps pro-

vide an understanding of the general shape of the buildings, how they will relate to one another, and how they will complement the features of the site and surroundings.

Once the agency accepts the concepts, the designers begin to prepare dimensional floor plans that illustrate all the spaces required for each program or function. These drawings indicate floor areas, specific space relationships and adjacencies, and methods of entry and exit between individual rooms or spaces and between buildings. Features such as special equipment are also identified. The design team reviews the design for compliance with zoning regulations, codes, and various standards. The budget is also reviewed and the cost estimate and construction schedule are revised as needed. Whenever the estimated cost or schedule is 5 to 10 percent above or below the budget or original schedule, the design team and agency should reconcile the differences as quickly as possible; otherwise these differences will magnify with time.

During the latter stages of the schematic design, as the general plan assumes a more understandable form, many people begin to relate to the project more easily than they could at earlier stages. Agency personnel often do not seriously engage in earlier design activities because of their unfamiliarity with the processes. Nonetheless, it is very important for them to be involved in each stage and to exercise their approval authority with full knowledge of the implications.

Design Development Phase

The design development phase further refines the architectural design, delineating the specific types of construction materials to be used, building forms, appearances, and exterior fenestration (windows). The mechanical, electrical, and security systems are defined, and outline specifications of all systems, materials, and construction techniques are prepared. The budget is reviewed again, and the construction cost estimate and schedule are updated.

The agency should carefully review all design developments and related documents prior to approval; significant changes or new directions given to the architect and engineers after this phase can be costly in both time and money.

Construction Documents Phase

During this phase the architect prepares working drawings, specifications, and, if appropriate, other bidding documents that will become components of the contract(s) between the agency and the construction contractor(s). Further refinements of the design are reviewed with the agency, including the quality and type of materials, equipment, and finishes required for all phases of the work.

When the construction documents are complete, a new cost estimate is prepared and the complete package is reviewed by the agency. This review is particularly important, since the documents will form a legally binding agreement between the agency and the contractor(s) and any subsequent changes are likely to be expensive.

Bidding and Negotiations Phase

Although private-sector clients will sometimes negotiate the cost of construction with one or more contractors and award a contract without competitive bidding, most public agencies require competitive bids.

Typically, the contract is awarded to the low bidder unless there is evidence that the low bidder is not qualified to do the work. Law or regulation may require that the agency conduct the contract bidding and award process; if so, the architectural and engineering team will play only a minimal role during this phase.

Construction Phase

Depending on the agency's policy, the architectural and engineering team may work closely with the project contractor(s) during the construction phase. This work usually includes such functions as approving shop drawings and payment requests, coordinating changes required in the design, observing the work in progress, and conducting substantial-completion and final-completion inspections of the project.

Client agencies sometimes contract with the architect for only a portion of these services. In other instances, the architect is asked to provide additional services, such as providing a full-time, on-site representative. Fees are adjusted accordingly.

CONSTRUCTION METHODS

Conventional Construction Contract

A conventional construction contract usually results from the agency advertising for contractors to submit cost proposals, or bids, for the complete construction of a planned project. The owner usually establishes time limits for completion of the work or else negotiates completion dates with potential contractors. After receiving the bids the owner evaluates the proposals and typically awards a contract to the lowest bidder unless that bidder fails to qualify; in such an event, the next lowest bidder or bidders are automatically considered until a qualified contractor is selected.

For all but the simplest projects, the bids submitted by general, or "prime," contractors are based on cost quotations from subcontractors who will do most of the work. A general contractor, once selected, is responsible for ensuring that each subcontractor meets his individual obligations and for coordinating all of the work to be performed. The general contractor also has responsibility to ensure that the project is completed within the agreed price and schedule.

Construction Management Method

Some agencies planning the construction of complex projects may not have sufficient in-house capability to schedule, coordinate, and manage the necessary planning, programming, design, and contract administration. In such cases, a construction manager or construction management firm may be hired as an agent of the owner to provide these services. Most construction managers have extensive contracting experience, in addition to their general administration skills, and their "contractor's" perspective can be very beneficial during the early planning and design stages.

The construction work is often subdivided into several contracts, with the construction manager responsible for many of the functions that ordinarily would be carried out by a general contractor.

This method of contract administration allocates the role that agency staff usually perform to an outside consultant or a team of consultants whose duties may include assisting the agency in hiring an architect and helping to coordinate and translate agency requirements into the design of the project.

Phased (Fast-Track) Construction Method

Phased, or fast-track, construction is a specialized multiple-contract procedure that compresses the amount of time needed to complete the construction of a project. When used successfully, it enables correctional agencies to complete facilities more quickly, an important consideration in the event of acute housing shortages, and may result in significant savings, especially during periods of high inflation.

Fast-track construction requires much more intensive planning, scheduling, and coordination than

To employ inmates successfully, it is essential that staff are skilled in the various building trades and adept at working with inmates. Designers should also plan a facility that uses easily erected construction components and relatively simple building techniques. Often, however, projects performed by inmates take much longer to complete, thereby offsetting some or even all of the cost savings.

other methods during both the design and construction phases. Instead of using a prime contractor, each phase of the construction process is bid separately. A construction management firm is usually engaged by the agency to coordinate these multiple contracts. The firm receives a fixed compensation from the agency for this service, and does not profit directly from getting the construction contractor's work accomplished. Since most construction management firms have substantial contracting experience, it is desirable to engage them early in the process so that they can work closely with the architect during the project design and the development of construction contract documents.

Fast-track construction compresses the work schedule by overlapping activities that otherwise would be performed sequentially. For example, as soon as the general design of the facility has been approved, the architect prepares contract documents for rough grading of the site. Once the grading contract is awarded, this phase of work commences while the rest of the design is being completed. Similarly, site work on utilities and foundations begins while the architect completes detailed design and construction documents on other phases of the project.

Because of the increased complexity of the architectural, engineering, and construction services involved, the agency can expect to pay substantially higher fees for the fast-track method. For projects that are good candidates for fast-tracking, the extra fees are more than offset by savings in construction costs and earlier completion of the work. One disadvantage of using this method is that it may be difficult or very costly to make significant changes during the latter stages of design even though the changes were necessitated by unforeseen circumstances.

Inmate Labor

A correctional agency may want to consider using inmate labor and in-house staff to construct some or all of the facility. This can provide meaningful work for inmates, reduce idleness, and eliminate the high cost of contract labor. Often, however, projects performed by inmates take much longer to complete, thereby offsetting some or even all of the cost savings.

To employ inmates successfully on these projects, it is essential that staff are skilled in the various building trades and adept at working with inmates. Designers should also plan a facility that uses easily erected construction components and relatively simple building techniques.

Several factors should be analyzed carefully before making a decision about the feasibility of using inmate labor:

- Distance of the inmate labor force from the construction site and on-site accommodations
- Type of work and skills required
- Number of skilled inmates available
- Inmates' custody or security requirements
- Availability of staff to supervise inmates
- Cost and time factors involved in use of inmate labor compared to non-inmate labor
- Effect of using inmate labor on local employment conditions
- Legal liability
- Equipment and material warranties
- Need for inmate employment.

The use of a construction management firm is common in projects as complex as a correctional facility, especially where fast-track construction techniques are being used. Where such assistance is being considered, it is best to engage the firm as early in the process as possible to take advantage of their expertise in the development of the contract documents.

Capacity of Facility and "Clustering"

Current standards recommend that institutions have a design capacity of no more than 500 inmates, primarily because programs at facilities this size or smaller can be conducted on a manageable scale. As the population in a facility exceeds this number, it becomes increasingly difficult to maintain a healthy atmosphere, promote open communications, provide programs tailored to individual needs, control tensions, and ensure the safety of both staff and inmates.

On occasion, correctional systems requiring large expansion programs have resorted to "clustering" two or more facilities on a common site, with each facility typically having a capacity for up to 500 inmates. There are two basic reasons for this strategy: 1) reduced direct capital and operating costs because of the economies of scale inherent in such a plan and the sharing of certain service functions, and 2) the difficulty of obtaining sites, particularly ones close to major urban centers.

Despite these rationales, decision-

GENERAL DESIGN AND CONSTRUCTION ISSUES

makers are urged to avoid clustering two or more institutions on a common site if possible. While the direct savings are apparent, the indirect costs, although not readily measurable, are substantial. The tendency to maximize direct savings often produces a "super-administration" and a "super-warden" with many of the problems inherent in older and larger institutions. If clustering of institu-

tions is planned, organizational structures and policies should be designed specifically to ensure that each facility's programs can function independently.

Staff Housing

Some correctional systems provide housing on the institutional grounds for key management staff and a number of line staff. One rationale for this practice is rooted in the past, when most correctional institutions were built in remote locations and adequate housing was unavailable in nearby communities. A second rationale is disturbance control. In the event of disturbances, it is important that additional personnel can be summoned to the institution on short notice, and the presence of staff near the institution provides an extra measure of security.

This text does not provide guidelines for housing staff at new institutions because the practice is being abandoned with increasing frequency. Most correctional systems try to locate new institutions closer to major communities where good housing is available near the facility. In addition, experience has shown that the

Despite these rationales, decision-makers are urged to avoid clustering two or more institutions on a common site if possible. While the direct savings are apparent, the indirect costs, although not readily measurable, are substantial.

private housing industry will respond to the demand for new housing created by a new employment base even in small communities. As long as good policies and procedures are developed for alerting off-duty staff during emergencies, in many cases it is no longer necessary to have employees reside at the facility. It is also generally healthier for staff and their families to live a normal life in nearby communities, sharing in civic responsibilities and enjoying social functions as regular members of the community.

Designers should review the issue of staff housing with the agency early in the planning process to determine if it is needed. The inclusion of staff housing has significant implications on, among other things, the budget, site requirements, utilities, and operating costs.

Landscaping

Landscaping should be an integral part of the overall design of any institution, including a correctional facility. Landscaping contributes to the non-institutional atmosphere desired of today's correctional facilities by "softening" their character. For the type of facility discussed in this book, the landscaping should be similar to that found on a small college campus, with maximum use made of existing plant material. The selection of additional plants, trees, and shrubs should be compatible with the site terrain and surrounding area. Ease of maintenance should also be considered. In developing the landscaping scheme, designers must pay careful attention to sight lines to ensure that views of the perimeter are not obscured and

that clear lines of vision are maintained to facilitate supervision of the compound from the control center and other staff offices. Landscaping can be used to direct traffic, and to provide places for people to assemble and gather. It is also a planning tool for establishing focal distances and obliterating vision to unsightly areas.

Site Plan Considerations
Throughout this guidebook, the proper location of various functions is described in terms of their interrelationships. Typically, suggestions for siting focus on the adjacencies of certain functions—how close they should be placed to one another and whether or not they should share a common border—as well as their location relative to major inmate circulation paths, principal staff routes, sally ports, truck docks, or service areas. Taken in total, these criteria will establish the overall organization of the functions in relationship to the site.

Designers must be conscious of the general configuration of buildings and their impact on supervision. Yet, with proper management and adequate staff, it is no longer necessary

Landscaping should be an integral part of the design. Attractive plantings can contribute significantly to the normal, hospitable atmosphere that the architectural design attempts to convey.

to align corridors and buildings in sterile configurations that enhance "universal surveillance" from a limited number of points. It is also counterproductive. The lack of sensory stimuli and the overbearing atmosphere of surveillance usually produced by designs that are overly concerned with security and custody only add to the tensions and stress of both staff and inmates.

The goal of site planning in relation to security should be to achieve a proper balance between good supervision and sound functional relationships in as normal an environment as is possible in an institutional setting.

Campus plans, versus corridor-system plans, are particularly appropriate for attaining that balance. Inmates in the general compound, for example, where the vast majority of outdoor traffic occurs, can be easily observed by many staff whose main responsibilities do not include direct supervision per se. In fact, several institutions built in recent years have been designed so that the warden or superintendent as well as other top staff can survey virtually all of the interior "campus," or main compound, from their offices. In these examples,

With increasing frequency, new institutions are designed with interiors that convey a less threatening and more humane atmosphere. Durable and reasonably priced furniture can be made of wood or plastic, sometimes in combination with metal parts (right). In some areas, such as the visiting room (left), upholstered furniture is appropriate.

Campus plans are particularly good for attaining a balance between the need for good supervision and sound functional relationships among spaces in the facility. For instance, inmates on the compound, where most circulation occurs, can be informally observed not only by correctional staff in the control center, but by other staff as they perform their regular duties.

the chief executive's office has been located on the second floor of the administration building where good public accessibility is maintained. Similarly, other top staff have been located on the second level, although not adjacent to the warden or the warden's immediate staff.

Likewise, the perimeter of buildings should reflect a balance between the functional design requirements of the spaces they enclose and the need for good supervision. It is not necessary, for example, that buildings have absolutely straight walls without recesses, so long as those recesses are visible by moving patrols.

Building roofs should be reasonably free of potential hiding places. This general requirement is imperative for structures that are part of the secure perimeter system—for example, an entrance structure that is aligned with the perimeter fence system and forms an integral element of the perimeter security system.

Furnishings

Many correctional institutions have been designed to include fixed, heavy-duty metal furniture in such areas as inmate rooms, dayrooms, gamerooms, and dining rooms. Dining and game tables have often been made of heavy-duty stainless steel with fixed steel stools. The underlying reason is to prevent inmates, who might be destructive, from easily damaging the furniture or using chairs or parts of heavier pieces as weapons during potential disturbances. Unfortunately, the environment created by such furnishings, coupled with architectural features such as barriers and the management style frequently accompanying these practices, actually contributes to the very behavior it is designed to protect against. Also, these furnishings are very costly.

With increasing frequency, new institutions are designed with interiors that convey less threatening, more humane atmospheres and with architectural surfaces that dampen noise. Articles of furniture that complement these interiors are important design features that must not be overlooked.

Durable and reasonably priced tables and chairs, in particular, can be made of wood or plastic, sometimes in combination with metal parts. In some areas, upholstered furniture such as sofas or benches may be appropriate. It is important to select materials that meet life safety codes, especially any foam materials used in chairs and sofas.

Wood butcher-block furniture, whether fixed or free, has been found surprisingly practical in certain applications. If well constructed, it shows less wear and tear than other more traditional materials. Painted furniture, for example, chips easily and quickly becomes unsightly. Butcher-block, on the other hand, does not suffer this problem and its appearance both initially and after prolonged use is much more pleasing. The only significant problem noticed with its use is marring caused by cigarette burns, but the appearance is far less objectionable than chipped paint and the burns can be sanded away periodically.

Without question, one of the biggest contributors to stress in correctional settings is inadequate noise control. In general, the furnishings and architectural treatment of inmate activity areas should be designed to reduce noise to the lowest possible levels. Acoustic tile and industrial-grade carpeting, for example, can be used in many areas without sacrificing either safety or security.

The goal of site planning in relation to security should be to achieve a proper balance between good supervision and sound functional relationships in as normal an environment as is possible in an institutional setting. Campus plans, versus corridor-system plans, are particularly appropriate for attaining that balance.

2
INMATE
HOUSING

Inmate housing is among the most important elements of any correctional facility. The type of housing provided conveys to the inmates the philosophy and general attitude of the administration and sets the tone for the entire facility. Housing must not only meet the security needs of the inmate population, but also meet standards of decency and humaneness. The housing design should strive to minimize the natural tensions and frustrations that result from confinement and institutional living. The design should create an atmosphere that fosters a feeling of self-worth and encourages inmates to use their period of confinement for personal growth and self-improvement.

Overcrowding has been a serious recurring phenomenon in most correctional systems throughout history. Many of these systems have been unable to address the issue adequately, primarily for lack of funds and public support. In recent years, the courts have increasingly intervened as a result of legal action taken by inmates, or on their behalf, and ruled that some conditions of confinement, including overcrowding in the living

GENERAL HOUSING

units of certain institutions, constitute cruel and unusual punishment.

The Supreme Court, in reviewing the findings of lower courts has not always agreed with them. In *Rhodes v. Chapman,* it found that overcrowding to the degree experienced in one Ohio institution did not of itself automatically support a finding of cruel and unusual punishment. Rather, it was ruled that all aspects of the living circumstances should be considered in determining the adequacy of conditions of confinement. Out-of-cell time, programs offered, rapport between inmates and staff, sanitation level, and newness of the

facility were some of the important considerations weighed in this case.

While this case may provide correctional administrators with some flexibility, the design of an institution should not include provisions to crowd living quarters. For instance, service facilities sized to accommodate a "crowded capacity" could cause staff and management to be more comfortable operating an over-crowded facility, even though the housing conditions were unsatisfactory. Such relative contentment could tend to delay necessary remedial action.

Inmate Rooms

Private rooms best meet the goals of decency and humaneness, and they provide more flexibility and better security. While the initial construction cost for private rooms is somewhat higher than that for multiple-occupancy housing, there are significant long-term advantages to this type of construction. Single rooms reduce the likelihood for conflict that occurs in multiple-occupancy housing. In the event of a disturbance, individual rooms substantially enhance the administration's ability to handle disruptive behavior by enabling the officer on duty to lock each inmate in his or her own room until the problem is resolved. This kind of control cannot be exercised in a dormitory or multiple-occupancy living arrangement. Thus, private rooms not only are more manageable and safer for both inmates and staff, but staff supervision costs may be lower. In addition, institutions with single rooms are more flexible in their ability to accommodate different types of inmates, a factor particularly important in view of the constantly changing characteristics of inmate populations during the life of a facility. Single rooms offer privacy, dignity, and personal space, which contributes to a more normal residential character and lessens management problems and attendant expenses.

Private rooms best meet the goals of decency and humaneness. Although initial construction cost for private rooms is somewhat higher than for multiple occupancy housing, there are significant long-term advantages—for instance, in privacy and security.

Decentralized Unit Management

A decentralized management system is recommended whereby an institution is subdivided into semi-autonomous units. The basic elements are as follows:

- Each unit comprises a relatively small number of inmates. Ideally, the size of units should range from 40 to 65 inmates. Since staff resources are often scarce, combining two units under one staff team is frequently necessary.

- Inmates are housed in the same unit for the major portion of their confinement.

- Inmates work in a close relationship with a multidisciplinary team of staff who are permanently assigned to the unit and whose offices are located in the unit.

- Staff members have decision-making authority for most aspects of institutional programming and living for the inmates assigned to them.

- Assignments to a particular unit are based on the inmate's need for the specific level of control or program offered in that unit.

Decentralized unit management increases contact between staff and inmates, fosters better interpersonal relationships, and leads to more knowledgeable decisionmaking as a direct result of staff dealing with smaller, more permanent groups of inmates. At the same time, the facility benefits from the economies inherent in centralized service facilities, including one food service facility, one clinic, one education and vocational training complex, and one gymnasium.

There are generally two types of units under the unit management concept: general units and special program units. The program in specialized units is tailored specifically to the common needs of the population housed in that unit. Depending on the needs of its inmates, an institution could have one or more specialized program units to serve inmates who could profit from such things as alcohol or other chemical abuse programs, or pre-release planning. The remaining units provide for general programs.

In an institution using a decentralized unit management system, newly admitted inmates are assigned to their

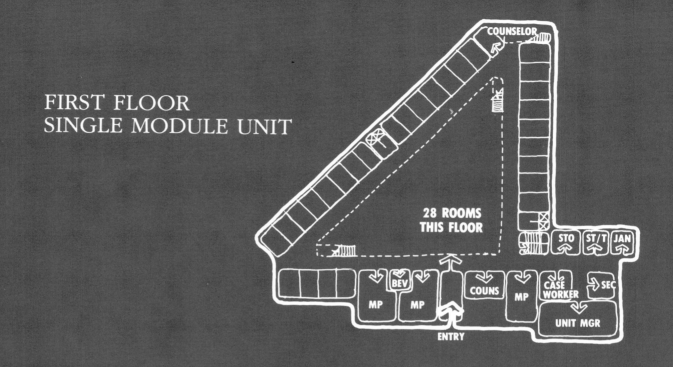

FIRST FLOOR
SINGLE MODULE UNIT

28 ROOMS
THIS FLOOR

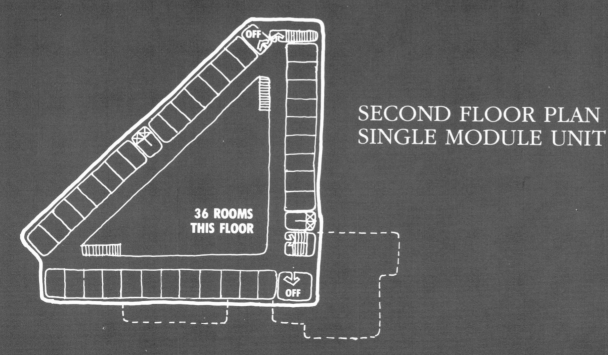

SECOND FLOOR PLAN
SINGLE MODULE UNIT

36 ROOMS
THIS FLOOR

FIRST FLOOR
DOUBLE MODULE UNIT

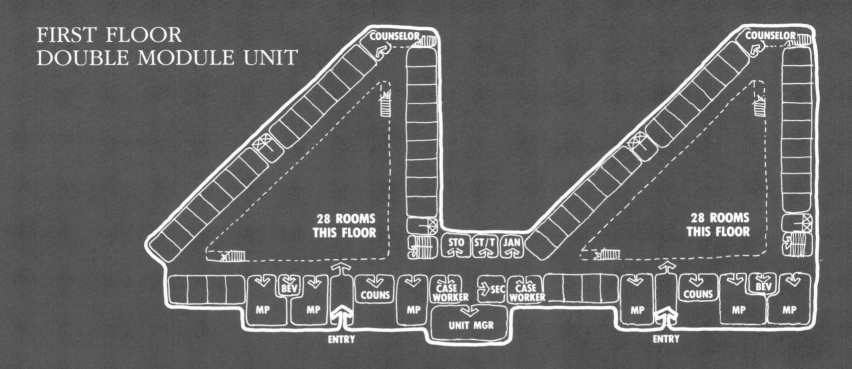

28 ROOMS
THIS FLOOR

COUNSELOR

28 ROOMS
THIS FLOOR

COUNSELOR

STO · ST/T · JAN

MP · BEV · MP · COUNS · MP · CASE WORKER · SEC · CASE WORKER · MP · COUNS · BEV · MP · MP

UNIT MGR

ENTRY   ENTRY

SECOND FLOOR
DOUBLE MODULE UNIT

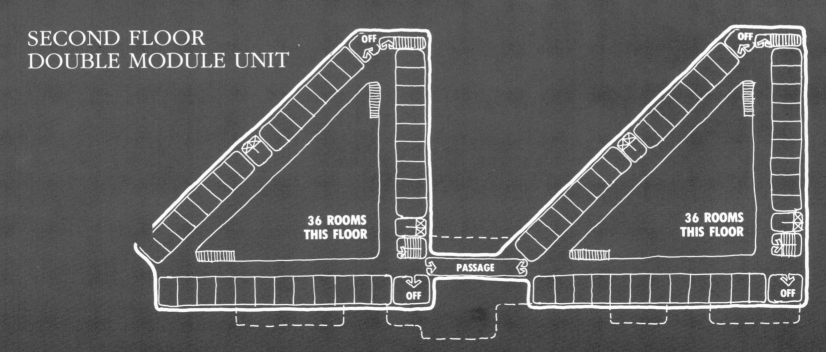

36 ROOMS
THIS FLOOR

36 ROOMS
THIS FLOOR

OFF   OFF

OFF   OFF

PASSAGE

unit after being processed through the admissions area. Inmate profile information obtained through presentence reports and other sources is analyzed to determine the appropriate unit assignment. In some facilities, at least one general unit is used to house inmates who are classified as predators (those who bully or prey on weaker inmates). Another general unit is used to house the weaker inmates who are susceptible to being preyed upon or victimized. It is desirable that there be at least one other general unit to which inmates who are neither predators nor potential victims can be assigned. If assigned judiciously, inmates from this "middle" group can also be housed in one of the "predator" or "victim" units to balance the populations of those units; however, under no circumstance should "weak" inmates be placed in units primarily for predators, or vice versa.

Offenders assigned to one of the general program units are sometimes moved at the discretion of the unit team into a special program unit. Such transfers should always be on a "round-trip ticket" basis—if the individual does not work out well in the special program unit, the inmate usually returns to the unit from which the transfer was made.

Unit Teams

A unit with a stable staff allows an offender's total correctional program plan to be designed and implemented by a single small, integrated group of staff members—the unit team. The unit team is multidisciplinary; for a unit of 40 to 65 inmates, there typically should be one unit manager, one caseworker, two counselors, and a secretary in addition to the correctional officers. If staff resources are low and a single unit of up to 130 inmates is created, it may be staffed by

one unit manager, one or two caseworkers, two or three counselors, and a secretary. In either case, the team is usually supplemented by part-time staff members such as education and mental health specialists.

The team is responsible for all aspects of inmate program planning and monitoring, including program assignments, implementation of treatment programs, coordination of leisure activities, participation in disciplinary hearings, making parole recommendations, and conducting prerelease programming. The team is also responsible for sanitation, the physical appearance of the unit, and custody and control of the inmates.

The unit is administered by a unit manager who is the direct-line supervisor of all staff assigned to the unit team, including the correctional officers. The unit manager represents the unit at institution-wide administrative meetings and usually reports to an assistant warden.

Circulation Patterns

Historically, inmate circulation between centralized program/service facilities and housing areas was confined to secure, enclosed corridors.

By placing correctional officer stations and staff offices within the housing units, frequent and direct contact between staff and inmates is encouraged. Supervision becomes a natural by-product of other inmate-related duties.

This arrangement provided maximum control of inmate movement. With more effective perimeter security and outdoor lighting systems, a "campus" plan is not only viable but desirable. A variety of outdoor walks or foot paths between the housing units and the central facilities is recommended in order to diffuse traffic, relieve congestion, and reduce the likelihood of conflict. Separate housing structures dispersed from one another and from major service and administrative functions offer great diversity, provide exercise, stimulate the senses, and help reduce the tensions inherent in institutional living. This more "normalized" environment ultimately contributes to the safety of both staff and inmates.

Conversely, tightly clustered facilities with their limited, congested, and often rigid inmate circulation routes contribute to management problems. They may appear to solve management problems because there is less area for staff to supervise; similarly, potential altercations may seem to be more observable and therefore controllable. But overly zealous attention to rigid, tight circulation is counterproductive and may

lead to a self-fulfilling prophecy that inmates are prone to disruptive behavior and violence and, as a consequence, must be closely watched. Institutions housing the most difficult-to-manage inmates may be an exception, and such facilities may need to be more tightly designed. To the extent possible, the major outdoor circulation routes should be visible from the institution's control center. Certain staff offices should also be located so that "casual supervision" of most circulation paths is a natural by-product of regular duties.

Housing structures should be far enough apart from one another so that the interior of rooms in one building cannot be viewed closely by inmates in other buildings. In addition, a minimum of 100 feet should be provided between the housing structures and the security fence; 125 to 150 feet is preferable. The resulting openness provides sufficient space

for proper supervision of the area.

In contemporary designs based on the unit management concept, the housing structure out of necessity is often composed of two modules of 40 to 65 inmates each. The two modules should be connected by corridors or a doorway that provide managers the flexibility to operate the modules either independently or as a combined unit. Even when the individual modules are operated autonomously, this arrangement enables nighttime supervision to be performed by a single officer observing both modules without going outside the building security.

Multi-use Area

The term "dayroom" traditionally has been used to describe the space in housing units devoted to general leisure-time activities such as watching television or playing table games. Usually, a single "dayroom" was

By placing correctional officer stations and staff offices within the housing units, frequent and direct contact between staff and inmates is encouraged. Supervision becomes a natural by-product of other inmate-related duties.

A variety of activity spaces should be provided in the housing units. The large multi-purpose room (above), has been broken by circular alcoves that enhance the feeling of privacy. Smaller rooms off the central multi-purpose use room (below), should be provided for games, listening to music, TV viewing, and other small group activities.

located near the entrance to the unit off the main circulation corridor along which inmate rooms were located. Such a configuration makes it difficult for the housing officer to supervise both the inmate rooms and the dayroom simultaneously. Some contemporary housing unit designs have adopted a plan that eliminates the single- and double-loaded corridors of inmate rooms and combines the normal "corridor" space with the normal "dayroom" space to create a central multi-use area around which all inmate rooms are grouped. This multi-use space eliminates the need for traditional corridors that have to be patrolled rigorously. Since each room opens directly onto the central area, staff can see the face of each door and into some rooms when the doors are open without having to move around very much in the central multi-use area. Surveillance by staff is improved to the extent that it seems almost casual, and becomes more a by-product of other important inmate management duties rather than the predominant concern.

To economize space and dollars and facilitate staff supervision, most contemporary housing designs that adopt the multi-use area approach locate the inmates' rooms on two tiers, creating a split-level scheme. This arrangement facilitates clear visibility to most, if not all, rooms. With proper classification, it is usually acceptable for a few rooms to be less visible if such an arrangement results in significant cost savings; such rooms are assigned to inmates who have proved to be reliable.

If the central multi-use space is carefully planned and large enough, and has sufficient sound-absorbing materials, one or more television sets can be placed in this space. Because of the high volume of noise that usually emanates from the sets it is often best to provide one or two small TV rooms adjacent to the area. Another small room, also adjacent to the central multi-use area, should be provided for quiet activities such as reading. Each of these small rooms should have large glassed partitions between them and the larger multi-use area. In addition to providing spaces for indoor recreation and other leisure activities, the multi-use areas are suitable for various unit meetings or other unit-wide activities.

In addition to the multi-use space in the housing units, many correctional facility designs include outdoor recreation space adjacent to each housing structure, usually a small, hard-surfaced half-basketball court. This space can serve a variety of recreational activities and offers inmates an opportunity for informal, unscheduled recreation.

Barriers

One of the most controversial issues in correctional facility design today concerns physical barriers that separate staff and inmates. Some authorities believe that secure mini-control rooms are required in each housing unit for all but minimum-security inmates. The staff assigned to these control rooms do not come into direct contact with inmates; instead, the officer operates doors to inmate rooms by remote control. The underlying assumption is that firm controls can be imposed quickly in periods of crisis without endangering staff or innocent inmates and that potential disturbances can be contained. But establishing barriers between staff and inmates, such as the mini-control rooms, promotes a staff attitude about inmates that too often

With more effective perimeter security and outdoor lighting systems, a "campus" plan is not only viable but desirable. A variety of outdoor walks or foot paths between the housing units and the central facilities is recommended in order to diffuse traffic, relieve congestion, and reduce the likelihood of conflict. Separate housing structures dispersed from one another and from major service and administrative functions offer great diversity, provide exercise, stimulate the senses, and help reduce the tensions inherent in institutional living.

produces the anticipated disruptive behavior, and strong physical controls indeed prove to be necessary. By eliminating barriers and having all available housing unit staff in frequent, direct contact with inmates, potential problems are usually diffused before they become serious. Staff who are properly suited to, and trained for, this role establish a rapport with enough inmates in the group to feel the emotional pulse of the unit and address petty issues before they fester and become explosive.

In contrast, correctional officers in mini-control stations can only observe activities in the unit, either positive or negative; they cannot supervise inmates directly. Placing officers behind barriers tends to promote complacency on the part of staff, since their duties consist of little more than being "button pushers." This sends out three signals within an institution using mini-control rooms:

- Allows inmates to control the living unit
- Fosters a we/they dichotomy
- Portrays correctional officers as "helpless" people

The issue of barriers should be carefully weighed in planning new correctional institutions. Barrier architecture is very costly for initial construction, and, if the same level of staff/inmate interaction as in a barrier-free design is provided, long-term operational costs are also much higher. These added costs are difficult to justify. Numerous barrier-free facilities have operated successfully for many years with an average number of staff, without the use of mini-control rooms and related devices. It is strongly recommended that all housing units be barrier-free, except, perhaps, those for the small percentage of inmates who truly require maximum security controls. If managers are totally opposed to adopting barrier-free designs, there is an alternative solution: Control rooms and other security features can be added rather easily at a later date as long as the initial construction plans allow for this contingency. It should be noted that there may be possible underlying legal questions attached to the use of barriers concerning the liability of a correctional officer who is unable to physically intervene during an inmate altercation,

such as a fight or an assault; the officer can only witness the incident, not control or prevent it.

Inmate housing structures should be constructed primarily of fire-resistant materials (refer to the National Fire Protection Association Life Safety Code). To obtain a residential character, some "soft" materials such as wood can be used in the housing units; wood, however, cannot compose a significant portion of the construction materials. There should be two primary entrances into the housing structure, one for each module, located so that traffic enters and exits directly into or very near the central multi-use space and staff offices. Additional emergency entrances/exits are required to meet life safety/fire codes.

Space Requirements

The following spaces should be provided for each of the two housing modules:

- Central Multi-use Space. To accommodate up to 60 to 65 inmates, the central multi-use space should contain at least 1,800 square feet, preferably more. This space serves as a recreation area and meeting room, as well as an area from which casual surveillance takes place. The area allowance above does not by itself satisfy minimum standard allowances for dayroom/leisure-time space; other leisure-time rooms, described below, are needed to meet the minimum standards.

- Inmate Rooms. Individual rooms should have from 60 to 80 square feet, and contain a water closet, lavatory, bed, desk, chair, bookshelves, and wardrobe. As discussed above, the individual rooms are often grouped around the central multi-use space in a two-tiered, split-level scheme. China toilet fixtures are recommended for all but maximum security facilities; their cost is less than 10 percent of the cost of stainless steel security fixtures, and experience has shown that expensive metal fixtures are not necessary for most types of facilities. It usually is not necessary to incorporate fixed room furnishings, except for maximum security facilities. Movable furniture offers the inmate some flexibility, is less institutional, and provides a modest opportunity for individual expression. Each inmate's room should have a secure window on an exterior wall that allows natural light into the room. To the extent possible, room windows should face away from the institution for added privacy and improved security. Ground fault interrupters (GFI's) should be provided for the electrical outlets to prevent shock or improper use of electricity.

- Showers. Eight individual showers should be provided in each module, grouped at different points to be convenient to the inmates. There should be showers on each floor. The showers should be easy to supervise yet provide for privacy, and have a separate space for drying. Standards require that the water to shower heads be thermostatically controlled.

- Office Space. It is recommended that sufficient office space be planned to allow each module to operate as a separate autonomous unit. Most offices should be located near the entrance to the module so that staff can easily monitor the traffic in and out of the building without being diverted from their primary duties. It is desirable to group together the

Individual rooms should have a lavatory, toilet, bed, desk, chair, bookshelves, and wardrobe.

Individual showers dispersed throughout the housing unit improve supervision and eliminate many of the problems associated with a communal shower.

two sets of offices for flexibility. If the administration decides to operate the two modules as a combined unit, this design can easily adapt to that type of operation. The following offices should be provided in each module.

Unit Manager's Office. One office containing approximately 120 square feet should be provided for the unit manager and appropriate files. In those units where inmate records are stored, provisions must be made to ensure adequate fire protection and security appropri-

ate for the security level of the inmates housed in the unit.

Caseworker's Office. One office, with about 100 square feet, provides adequate room for the caseworker and necessary files, as well as space to talk privately with inmates.

Counselors' Offices. Each of the two counselors should have a private office for consultations with inmates. The offices should provide the same amount of space as a caseworker. For better supervision, these offices are sometimes

scattered throughout the module.

Correctional Officer's Station. An area of about 20 square feet, usually equipped with a stand-up desk and a telephone, should be provided in the central multi-use space.

Secretary's Office. A space with about 150 square feet should be provided for the secretary and unit records.

Other Offices. The unit should contain two additional offices of approximately 100 square feet each to be shared by staff who do not work in the unit all of the time, such as psychologists, chaplains, and teachers.

- Other Multi-use Rooms. In addition to the central multi-use space, the unit should contain approximately three rooms that also serve as multi-purpose spaces. These rooms should be different sizes, for example, two rooms of 150 square feet each and one room of approximately 300 square feet. The rooms should be located off the central multi-use area for easy supervision. At least one room should be used for television viewing to control the high noise levels

Offices for counselors and part-time specialists can be dispersed throughout the unit.

of that activity. If the budget permits, an additional television room is desirable to reduce inmate conflicts over program viewing preferences. (Televisions should be considered management tools, not merely amenities for the inmates.)

- Beverage Alcove. An area of about 80 square feet should be located off the central multi-use area. A drinking fountain with hot water dispenser, soft drink cooler, ice machine, and storage should be incorporated in the station.
- Telephone Area. Two stations, each equipped with a telephone for inmate use, should be adjacent to or part of the central multi-use space. Only collect calls can be made from these telephones.
- Storage Rooms. Two rooms, each about 50 square feet, should be provided for supplies and equipment.
- Janitor's Closet. Two janitor's closets should be provided, one on each floor, located near inmate rooms.
- Toilet. A restroom equipped with a water closet and lavatory should be located near staff areas for use by staff and visitors.

At least two private telephone stations for inmate use from which collect calls may be placed are recommended for each unit.

SEGREGATED HOUSING

Whether for disciplinary or security reasons, it is sometimes necessary for correctional administrators to separate some inmates from the main population. This period of confinement can vary from a few days to months. The general term used to refer to this type of housing is "segregation" (see ACA Standards 2-4214 to 2-4237). Segregated housing is used to detain inmates who are being investigated for rule infractions, those who are being punished for violating institution rules, and those who would be in danger if they were housed with the main population.

The movement of inmates housed in segregation is sharply restricted and controlled. Most activities take place in the segregation building. For example, meals prepared in the main kitchen are delivered to the segregation unit and served to the inmates in their rooms. Segregated inmates can usually receive visitors in the visiting room, but they must be escorted to and from that area. If their behavior is unpredictable, they may use the private visiting areas located in the main visiting room.

The segregation building is super-vised by security staff. Two officers are usually needed to operate these units during the day. Daily visits must be made by medical staff to check on the health of each inmate. Inmates' caseworkers and counselors from their regular housing units visit with inmates regularly for counseling. Other staff assist during special activities such as exercise periods. Good practice also requires that the warden and other administrative staff frequently inspect the units' program and operation.

Administrative Segregation and Disciplinary Detention. Administrative segregation generally refers to the separate housing provided inmates from the main population who, among other things, are being investigated for rule infractions. Except for restricted movement, these inmates are afforded the same privileges given inmates in the main population, including visiting, canteen, mail, education, library, and religious services.

In general, inmates are placed in disciplinary detention for a rule violation only after receiving a hearing by the institution's disciplinary committee. Disciplinary detention should be separate from the area designated as administrative segregation. Most inmates are usually confined to disciplinary detention for relatively short periods of time, but they remain in their rooms or cells most of the day, except for such activities as exercise, visiting, and appearances before committees for hearings and reviews. According to ACA standards, inmates in disciplinary detention are extended the same rights and privileges as inmates in administrative segregation with two exceptions: First, unless otherwise authorized by the chief executive officer, their telephone privileges are restricted except for those related to access to the inmate's attorney; and,

The segregation housing recommended is designed as a single structure composed of two wings, one housing administrative segregation inmates, the other housing the disciplinary detention population. Housing these two populations in a single building conserves resources by the sharing of staff and space such as offices, recreation, and multi-use areas.

Individual rooms in the segregation unit should be of secure construction. They should be equipped with security light fixtures, ground-fault-interrupter electrical outlets, and security toilet fixtures.

second, access to counseling, education, library services, and other programs is not required. Like inmates in administrative segregation, however, they must have access to such services as legal and other reading materials, medical care, mail, and basic personal and canteen items.

Segregation housing should be located away from major circulation paths, general inmate housing, and the parking lot. It is best located near the medical facility; standards require medical staff to check inmates in segregated housing daily, and the medical facility typically is not on a major inmate circulation path. Designers should pay particular attention to the orientation of the building; individual inmate rooms should not face the center of the compound where the general inmate population frequently crosses or the "front" of the institution where visitors enter. If the windows of inmates' rooms do face other nearby inmate housing or activities, an appropriate visual shield should be integrated into the design; earth berms are sometimes used for this purpose.

The segregation housing recommended on page 57 is designed as a single structure composed of two wings, one housing administrative segregation inmates, the other housing the disciplinary detention population. Housing these two populations in a single building conserves resources by the sharing of staff and space such as offices, recreation, and multi-use areas. Although the two populations can be housed in separate structures, this approach would require expensive duplication of space and staff.

Unlike general housing, there is no need for a large, central multi-use space in a segregation building because inmates are confined to their rooms most of the time and are not allowed to congregate. There is also no office space for a unit manager, caseworker, or counselors; since inmates are housed in segregation only temporarily, caseworkers or counselors from their original unit visit with them in the segregation building, using the hearing room or one of the small multi-use spaces.

The following spaces are included in the segregation building:

Sally Port. A 60-square-foot sally port should be provided as a security entrance into the segregation housing facility. The outer door is operated by the control center based on both audio intercom recognition and visual recognition through the use of closed circuit television. The inner sally port door is opened manually by a segregation unit officer or remotely by the control center officer.

Office. An office of approximately 120 square feet should be provided for the correctional officers, situated to provide a clear view of the sally port and major circulation within the building. If possible, it should also have a good view of the outdoor recreation yard.

Individual Rooms. For a facility of up to 500 inmates, a unit containing approximately 20 rooms for administrative segregation and 10 rooms for disciplinary detention is often sufficient. The rooms should be secure (see Building Security) and have at least 80 square feet to meet ACA standards. All rooms should be equipped with security light fixtures and ground-fault-interrupter electrical outlets, and most should be equipped with security toilet fixtures. Ideally, all rooms should be located on one level, although sometimes each wing is designed as a split-level, tow-tiered scheme.

Multi-use Rooms. Two rooms, of approximately 150 square feet each, should be located near the front of the building to serve as multi-use space.

Hearing Room. A centrally located hearing room of about 250 square feet serves the administrative segregation population and provides another multi-use room for either population.

Counseling/Interview Room. A room of approximately 100 square feet should be provided to enable program and other staff to talk with inmates privately. This room should

The officers' station in the segregation unit should have a clear view of all major circulation areas including the sally port and outdoor recreation.

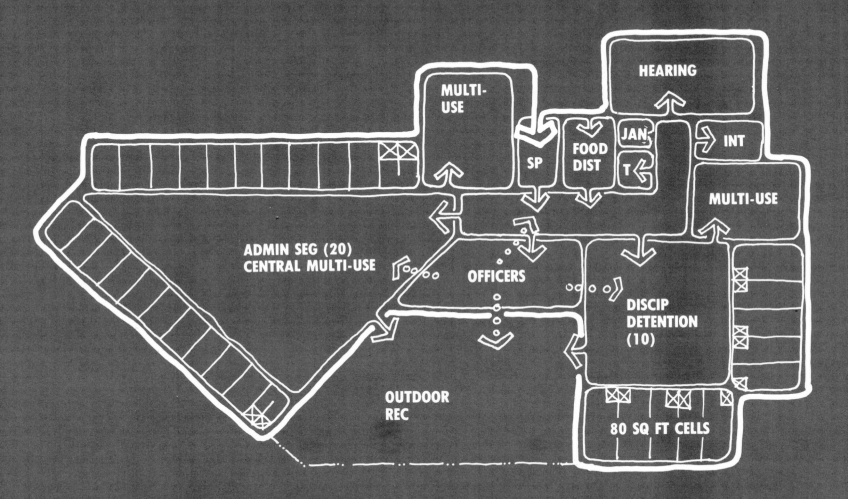

ADMINISTRATIVE SEGMENT/
DISCIPLINARY DETENTION

be located near the front of the building and be accessible to either population.

Toilet/Janitor's Closet. A small facility for staff and visitors should be provided.

Meal Distribution Area. Meals are distributed from a centrally located room of about 100 square feet that is equipped with a small refrigerator/freezer, microwave oven, counterspace, sink, and storage. Food is brought from the main kitchen in carts and, if appropriate, heated before being served.

Storage Room. A room of about 80 square feet is useful.

Outside Recreation Area. A secure outside area of approximately 2,500 square feet should be provided as recreation space for either population housed in this building. Use of this area should be scheduled to avoid mixing the populations. The recreation area should be located so that the inmates using this space can not be easily seen by the general population inmates or by visitors. A location that allows casual supervision from staff offices is recommended.

Showers. Experience has shown that inmates in disciplinary detention status are more difficult to manage than those in administrative segregation. Therefore it is recommended that each disciplinary detention room be equipped with a shower. Even though there is added initial cost, the life-cycle cost will be lower if staff efficiency and control are considered. This provision requires a total room area of at least 90 square feet. A group of three showers is sufficient for the 20 inmates in the administrative segregation wing; each shower should be single-occupancy with an adjoining drying area.

Telephones. Moveable or portable phone capability should be pro-vided to allow inmates to make phone calls from their cells. A mobile phone unit, wall jacks, or sufficiently long phone lines are alternatives to prevent unnecessary movement of inmates.

Protective Custody. The third major category of segregated housing is protective custody. Inmates generally are placed in protective custody because they would be in danger if they remained in the general population. If jurisdictions have only a few inmates requiring protective custody for short periods of time, it may be appropriate to place these inmates in the administrative segregation unit. Protective custody inmates, like the administrative segregation popula-

Since inmates take their meals in their rooms in the segregation unit, space to prepare food trays is necessary.

tion, should not be denied any of the rights or privileges allowed the general population.

Before placing an inmate in protective custody, the agency should explore the possibility of transfer to another institution or jurisdiction where the inmate could be housed safely in a general population. If transfers are not possible, and there are a substantial number of long-term protective custody cases in the system, consideration should then be given to the construction of a separate self-contained protective custody unit or, in some instances, the construction or designation of an entire institution for protective custody inmates.

The protective custody unit should incorporate the same features discussed previously for the segregation building. In addition, since protective custody inmates virtually never go to the main institution where they can be seen by general population inmates or members of the public, a separate protective custody unit in a general population institution must incorporate space for many of the activities that are provided centrally for the general population. These include an admission and discharge area, medical treatment/examination room, visiting area, dining space, vocational and education program, hair care service, and recreational facilities. Most other

services such as laundry and canteen can be processed centrally and the items themselves delivered to the protective custody inmates. Some services such as dental care in the medical facility would require the removal of other inmates from that area.

In extreme protective custody cases, such as witness protection, one solution is to create an autonomous unit equipped with all services needed to operate independently from the main institution except for administrative functions such as business and personnel activities. Such a unit would have independent pedestrian and vehicular sally ports at the perimeter fence, a separate control center, and would be equipped with separate laundry and food preparation facilities. The unit would be located near the fence, and all traffic in and out of the unit would originate outside the security of the main institution. This type of program obviously requires additional manpower and other resources; for additional information concerning this program, see the ACA protective custody manual.

In the administrative segregation wing, three individual showers with separate drying areas are recommended.

**3
INMATE
SERVICES**

The admissions activity comprises the orderly receiving, identification, and initial screening of all new inmates entering the facility. The inmate is usually anxious during this time; consequently, it is important that the admissions area convey a calm, pleasant, and orderly atmosphere.

When inmates enter, they may be placed in a holding area until the staff can begin the admissions process. During admissions, inmates are fingerprinted, photographed, and given forms to complete that will become part of their institution file. They are also issued a set of institutional clothing and provided with information about the institution's rules and procedures. Since a limited amount of personal belongings are permitted in the institution, an inventory of these items is made and items not permitted are stored in the personal property storage area until the inmate's release or, preferably, are mailed to the inmate's family.

Typically, the inmate's records are being reviewed to determine the appropriate housing assignment while the inmate is being processed for admission. When all the forms are

ADMISSIONS AND DISCHARGE

complete, a file is assembled and retained in the information management office, which ideally is located near the admissions and discharge area (see Chapter V, "Information Management and Research").

Standards require that all new admissions receive a thorough medical screening (see Appendix 2, 2-4290). Depending on the institution's practices, this exam may be given before inmates go to their assigned unit or as soon as possible thereafter.

To conserve staff and space, it is desirable to conduct all admissions and discharge activities in the same area. Discharge refers not only to inmates who have completed their sentence, but also other departures from the facility, including furloughs, staff-escorted day trips, court appearances, medical appointments, and work or study release. The discharge unit reviews all aspects of the inmate's departure and assembles the necessary records and information. Discharge duties include verification of release orders, inmate identification, funds clearance, medical clearance, determination of transportation needs, return of all governmental property, and verification of forwarding address. To eliminate any confusion, separate times should be designated for admission and discharge activities. If this cannot be arranged, then the holding rooms can be used to hold departing inmates while new admissions are being processed, and vice versa.

The admissions and discharge function is usually supervised by the security staff, with the number of staff determined by the intake, trans-

The admissions and discharge area is located inside the institution's secure perimeter near the front pedestrian sally port. The program functions most efficiently if it is also near the medical facility, mail room, and information management office—areas related to admissions and discharge activities.

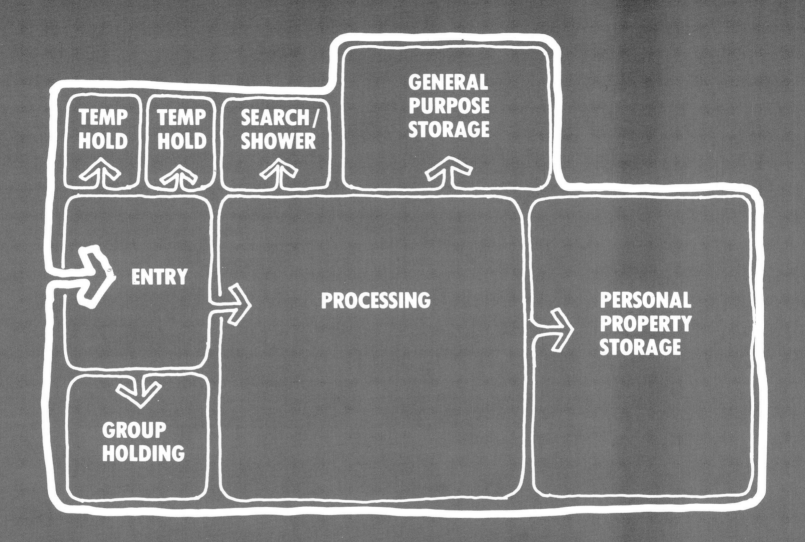

ADMISSIONS AND DISCHARGE

fer, and release volume. For a facility of this size, one officer is assigned full-time to the activity and receives assistance from other staff members as needed.

The admissions and discharge area is located inside the institution's secure perimeter near the front pedestrian sally port. The program functions most efficiently if it is also near the medical facility, mail room, and information management office—areas related to admissions and discharge activities. It is best that the path between the admissions/discharge area and the front sally port diverge from the traffic paths to the administration area, the visiting room, or other parts of the facility.

Entry. Inmates should enter the admissions/discharge area through a small vestibule that leads directly to the holding rooms. The entry should accommodate about six people comfortably.

Processing Area. A 400-square-foot processing area forms the nucleus of the admissions and discharge function. The area contains a station where staff process necessary forms and take fingerprints and photographs. The design should enable staff in the main activity area to see the entry vestibule and doors to the holding rooms as well as the search and shower area.

Holding Rooms. These rooms are used to temporarily hold inmates awaiting processing or transfer to their designated housing unit. They also are used for inmates being released and awaiting transportation. As newly arriving inmates are often anxious and sometimes disorderly or even violent, the rooms should contain a secure combination lavatory/water closet fixture and a secure light fixture. For a facility for 500 inmates, it is generally recommended that there be three holding rooms: two single-person rooms, each with about 80 square feet, and one multi-person room with approximately 200 square feet. The holding rooms should be constructed with view windows so that staff can easily observe inmate activity.

Search and Shower Area. This is usually a semiprivate alcove, located adjacent to the processing area and comprising a dressing area, shower, and toilet; 65 square feet is usually adequate for this area.

Personal Property Storage. This room should also be located adjacent to the processing area and should be equipped with storage shelves or lockers. The size of the room will vary according to the institution's policy defining the amount of personal property inmates can store at the institution. If the policy is stringent, the room may range from 200 to 400 square feet. If the policy is very liberal, from 1,500 to 2,000 square feet may be needed, which will add substantially to the capital costs.

General Purpose Storage. An area of about 200 square feet is needed to store forms and other supplies, as well as a small supply of the clothing issued to inmates during the admissions process. The area should be directly accessible from the processing area.

Since the behavior of incoming inmates is sometimes unpredictable, holding rooms in the admissions area should have view windows so that staff can easily see into the rooms.

Health care services that provide for inmates' physical and mental well-being must be offered and should include health education as well as medical, dental, mental health, nursing, personal hygiene, and dietary services. Quality health care depends on the combination of a qualified staff, an adequately equipped institutional medical facility, and contracts with resources in the community.

Because of the rising level of sophistication in medical care, the use of existing services in the community is increasingly important for providing comprehensive health care. One of the primary issues in designing the institution's medical facility is defining the level of care that can be provided through local contracts. Planners should determine what resources are available and assess the costs and benefits of providing certain services in-house vis-a-vis using community medical facilities.

If the institution contracts for services with local hospitals, the hospitals should be fully licensed and accredited. Similarly, any services provided by the correctional facility must meet the same legal require-

MEDICAL FACILITY

ments that a licensed medical facility must meet. Planners should consult the standards promulgated by organizations such as state health departments and the American Correctional Association to assure compliance with professionally accepted practices.

A complete health care file should be maintained for each inmate to accurately document all health care services provided during confinement. These records should be maintained in accordance with agency rules relating to security and privacy, and they should be retained for several years after an inmate's release, or as re-

quired by state law, to provide a record of treatment.

Inmate health services should begin with a physical and dental examination for all new inmates soon after their arrival at the institution. Psychological testing is usually conducted at this time as well. As part of a preventive health care program, new inmates also should receive any necessary immunizations.

The institution should establish a daily sick call during which inmates can report to the medical facility to consult a doctor or dentist, have x-rays or laboratory work, or pick up prescriptions. A daily sick call and medications must also be provided to inmates in segregation.

The clinic staff represents a variety of disciplines and should include a physician, a dentist, an administrator, nurses, physician assistants, a pharmacist, a laboratory technician, a psychologist, and clerks. Inmates should not be used in direct patient care or in the inmate records department where privacy and confidentiality of patients' records must be maintained, although carefully selected and trained inmates can be used in some roles such as housekeeping.

The medical facility should include spaces for diagnostic services including an X-ray room and a small laboratory for

The type of medical operation outlined in this text assumes that major medical/surgical procedures are available to the institution through contracts with community health services or at a specialized state or local medical facility. The following guidelines are designed for a clinic-type operation, with eight inpatient beds to care for inmates who are convalescing or who have minor illnesses yet are too ill to remain in their housing units.

The medical facility should be accessible to inmates but situated away from routine inmate or staff traffic. Ideally, it should be close to both the admissions/discharge unit and the segregation unit. This arrangement facilitates the delivery of routine entry and exit medical exams and the daily health care monitoring of inmates in segregation. Access to the facility by emergency vehicles and stretchers is essential.

Typically, a clinic of this type requires approximately 4,300 square feet and should be divided into the following functional areas.

Administration. A private office of about 120 square feet should be provided for the clinic administrator. A second office should be located adjacently to provide space for two clerks and for maintaining and storing all medical records; 400 square feet is usually sufficient for this purpose.

Diagnostic Services. This area includes a small medical laboratory of about 150 square feet for performing routine tests, including urinalysis procedures. A separate, shielded medical x-ray room of approximately 175 square feet is needed for diagnostic purposes. The use of an automatic x-ray film processing machine is recommended because it can be placed in the same room with the x-ray machine, eliminating the need for a separate darkroom.

Pharmacy. A pharmacy located near or adjacent to the outpatient waiting area eliminates unnecessary inmate traffic through other parts of the clinic and is also convenient for staff. It should occupy about 150 square feet, be designed to dispense drugs easily yet preclude inmate access to medications not authorized to them, and provide both refrigerated and non-refrigerated storage, including secure storage for controlled substances—a safe is usually provided for this purpose. All procedures and storage provisions should be conducted under the supervision of a certified pharmacist or in accordance with governing codes, or both. It is very important that walls, ceilings, floors, windows, and doors be sufficiently secure to prevent unauthorized access to medications stored there.

Outpatient Clinic. A waiting area with at least 150 square feet should be located at the entrance to the clinic. This area is used by inmates reporting for sick call and

The bulk storage area and pharmacy must be of secure construction. A safe for the storage of controlled drugs is recommended.

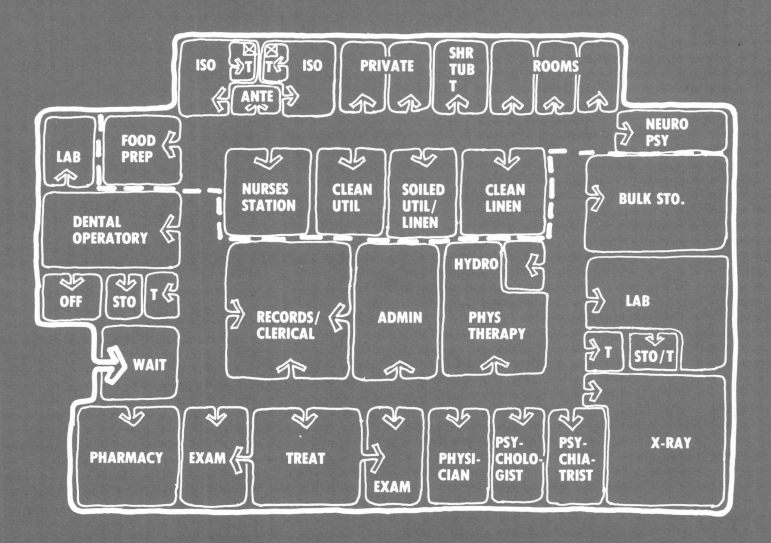

MEDICAL

should be equipped with a small station for a correctional officer to supervise the inmates and the general traffic. Direct access should be available to the medical records clerk, pharmacy, dental unit, and examination and treatment rooms.

Two examination rooms, each with 120 square feet, should be provided for a facility for up to 500 inmates. Privacy for both inmates and staff is necessary. The appropriate equipment will depend on the level of in-house care provided.

Treatment Room. A treatment room occupying 200 square feet should be located between the two examination rooms. It should be designed to permit minor surgical procedures and such activities as the use of respirators and EKG machines.

The following facilities are also required:
- A physician's office of about 150 square feet, for consultations and recording medical histories and treatment.
- A physical therapy room of approximately 160 square feet, used by inmates primarily for hydrotherapy. Designers should determine the types of physical ther-apy planned for the new facility and size and equip the room appropriately.
- A bulk storage room of about 250 square feet, for storing assorted supplies and equipment. This room should be securely designed to prevent unauthorized access to medical supplies.
- A janitor's closet.
- Two toilet rooms for use by staff, visitors, and inmates. One room should be located near the x-ray room and equipped for the handicapped; the other should be located near the waiting area.

Dental Care. A small but comprehensive dental suite is needed in virtually all correctional facilities in order to provide inmates with ade-quate dental health care. Services include screening, preventive hygiene, examinations, and treatment. Either in-house professional staff, or purchase-of-services contract staff, or both, can provide the necessary professional services. While some designs place all services within one open room with screen partitioning, the preferred method is to provide separate rooms clustered around a dental operating room. This method requires the following facilities:
- A dental operating room of approximately 250 square feet for routine examination and treatment, incuding oral surgery. This area is usually equipped with two dental stations, or chairs, and a wall-mounted dental x-ray unit,

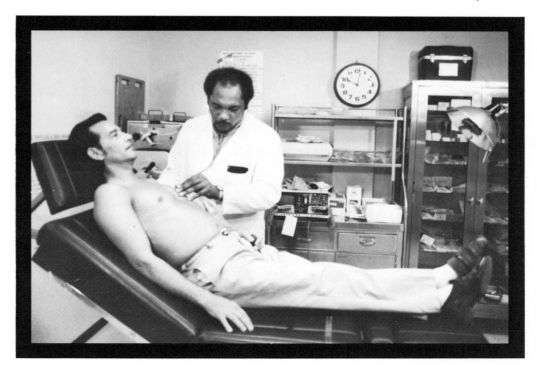

Two examination rooms and a treatment room for routine medical procedures should be sufficient in a facility for 500 inmates.

which should be accessible to both stations. If only one dental station is needed, 175 square feet of space will be sufficient.

- A dental laboratory for performing routine tests and preparing materials to be used in the dental treatment areas. Generally, 150 square feet is adequate. If technicians will be preparing dentures, or if dental training for inmates is planned, a space of at least 250 square feet should be provided.

- A storage space of about 50 square feet for equipment and supplies used in the dental lab and operating room.

- A dentist's office of approximately 100 square feet for keeping records, maintaining reference materials, and consulting with inmates.

Inpatient Area. Inpatient care is a distinct function within the medical facility, comprising rooms for patients as well as a nursing station, food preparation area, shower, and storage areas for clean and dirty linens and utensils. The inpatient area should be a secure, self-contained unit, designed so that it can be "locked off" from the outpatient function when that area is not being used.

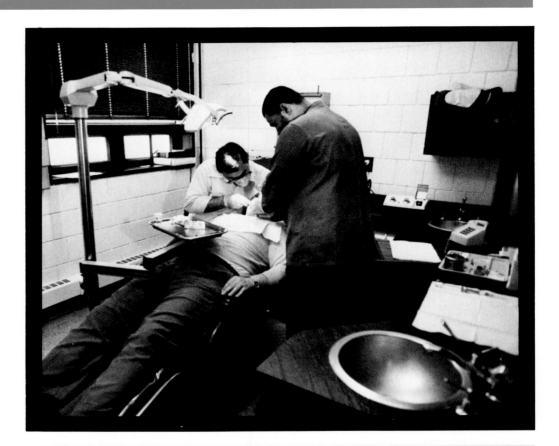

A small but comprehensive dental suite (above) is needed to provide adequate dental care. Spaces should include a dental operating room, laboratory, office, and storage room. The in-patient area (below) should be secure and self-contained so that it can be locked off at night or when not in use.

Five private inpatient rooms should be available for inmates who require continuous care and supervision. The rooms should be monitored with an electronic nurse-call system and supervised by a staff member. If appropriate staff are not available, inpatient care is often provided in nearby community hospitals through contract arrangements.

A nursing station, or alcove, of about 80 square feet provides space for the staff member to supervise and operate the inpatient area. A work station with counter and storage space is typical. A secure, locked cabinet for daily medicine is suggested.

Two medical isolation rooms, each usually 130 square feet and equipped with a private shower, should be used to quarantine inmates with infectious diseases. Each room also requires an entry/exit vestibule of an additional 30 square feet equipped with a wash basin for visitor and staff use to prevent the spread of disease.

A food preparation area of approximately 100 square feet provides facilities for reheating and serving food to inmates confined in the infirmary. This area should be equipped with a microwave oven, sink, refrigerator, and counter and storage space for utensils and supplies that do not have to be returned to the main food service area.

A bathroom with a single shower, bathtub, and toilet should be provided for ambulatory patients.

Three separate rooms are needed for storing linens and utensils: a clean-linen storage room of about 75 square feet; a clean-utility room of about 100 square feet for storing utensils and equipment; and a combination soiled utility/linen room containing about 150 square feet. This third room is used for the temporary storage of soiled linens, utensils, and equipment that require cleaning or sterilization before reuse and should be equipped with an autoclave.

Mental Health. Part of the pre-design planning process for an institution involves an assessment of the mental health problems of the projected inmate population. Once a mental health profile has been developed, planners can decide on the level of care to be provided in-house and the extent to which existing mental health facilities in the community can be used. These issues will determine the type of space provided for this program as well as the type and level of staffing.

A facility for 500 inmates will house a wide range of mental health problems. Some inmates will display severe mental illness and need intensive care. Others may not be classified as mentally disturbed but will have psychological problems that interfere with their level of daily functioning. Consequently, there is a need to differentiate between inmates who require more intensive mental health assistance and those for whom less concentrated effort is warranted.

Some correctional systems cooperate with their local mental health departments to provide outside placement for severely disturbed inmates. If the jurisdiction does plan to house severely disturbed inmates in a

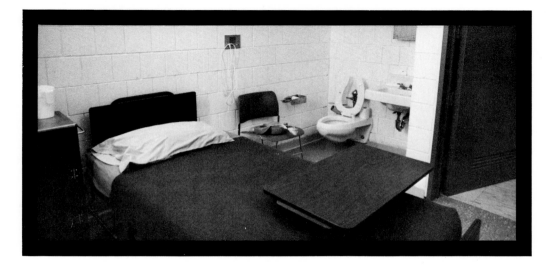

Private rooms are recommended for the inpatient area. In addition, two isolation rooms, each with a private shower and an entrance/exit vestibule, should be provided to quarantine inmates with infectious diseases.

correctional facility, they should not be housed with the general population, and a separate autonomous housing unit should be designated specifically for these inmates.

The mental health program discussed below assumes that inmates with serious, chronic mental health problems will be housed in a state or local mental health facility or a correctional facility specifically designed to care for such persons. It also assumes that inmates with less severe mental health problems who are housed in a regular housing unit will be seen by mental health staff on a regular basis. Many correctional systems employ part-time or consultant psychiatrists and rely on full-time psychologists to provide this needed day-to-day treatment.

To provide mental health services for inmates with moderate mental health problems, a facility of this size should be staffed with two psychologists and one clerk. The area may also temporarily house those inmates with more serious problems. If it is anticipated that severely mentally disturbed inmates will be housed at the facility, additional mental health personnel, and spaces will be needed

(occupational therapists, psychiatric nurses, and psychiatric social workers).

Mental health services staff need adequate work space and support staff to perform their duties. Each full-time mental health staff member should have an individual office in which privacy is assured.

Space is needed within the facility to temporarily house inmates suspected of severe mental health disorders who are awaiting transfer, or those whose behavior suggests they pose a danger to themselves or others. In designing this area, planners must carefully consider reducing the potential for inmate suicides.

Appropriate space is also needed for conducting group testing and private interviews. One of the classrooms or multi-use spaces near the auditorium can be used for these purposes, however, as can one of the small multi-purpose interview or meeting rooms provided in each housing unit.

If the mental health program is operated essentially as an outpatient program, only the following special areas are required, located in the medical facility:

- A single neuropsychiatric room of approximately 100 square feet should be used to isolate inmates whose violent behavior may endanger themselves or others, or those suspected of severe mental disorders who are awaiting transfer to a long-term mental health facility. This space should be adjacent to the medical services area so that medically trained staff are available at all times. All sharp surfaces and edges should be eliminated to ensure the patients' safety.

- Private offices, each occupying 150 square feet, should be provided for psychiatrists, psychologists or other mental health professionals for maintaining records and consulting with inmates. These offices should be located adjacent to the waiting room and near the outpatient area. At least two offices are recommended. If the level of mental health services to be provided will require more than two psychiatrists or psychologists, then additional offices will be necessary. Clerical staff located in the medical facility provide support to the psychiatrists and psychologists.

If the institution contracts for services with local hospitals, the hospitals should be fully licensed and accredited. Similarly, any services provided by the correctional facility must meet the same legal requirements that a licensed medical facility must meet. Planners should consult the standards promulgated by organizations such as state health departments, and the American Correctional Association to assure compliance with professionally accepted practices.

Few programs affect the climate of an institution more than its food service program. Moreover, a good food program is essential to the orderliness and safety of a correctional facility. When the food program is unsatisfactory, other problems often become magnified and disturbances are more likely to erupt. But a sound and appealing food service program—with appetizing, nutritional means prepared under sanitary conditions and attractively presented—will lessen the urgency of many inmate concerns.

The food service program should be supervised by an administrator. Other staff usually include a full-time assistant, cook supervisors, a baker, and relief staff. In addition, a large number of inmates customarily work in this area, although contract staff sometimes provide this service. The dining room is usually supervised by a combination of food service and security personnel.

Dining Area

Except for special housing programs such as the medical and segregation units, a single, central dining area is preferable to either

FOOD SERVICE

separate dining facilities in each housing unit or inmates taking their meals in their rooms. Inmates look forward to meals as a social time, which group dining enhances, and as a break from the routine of institutionalized living. Except, perhaps, for true maximum security facilities, group dining is also easier to manage and requires less staff, space, and equipment than other dining arrangements.

For the special housing programs, it has been a traditional practice to prepare the food in bulk in the main kitchen and transport it in bulk food carts to the special units, where it is served on individual trays or plates. Although this system remains in wide use, an increasingly popular method is to pre-plate the food in the main kitchen, transport it to the units in special carts, and then heat the "hot" dishes in microwave ovens before serving them. This method more likely assures that "hot" dishes are indeed hot when received by the inmates. It is also easier to manage and more sanitary than the traditional method. Appropriate transport cards are needed to keep the food cold and protected from contamination. In addition, a small food service room, or station, is needed in each unit where food is served. Each station should be equipped with a microwave oven, a small refrigerator, and a counter with a sink and storage space.

Staff in most correctional institutions take their meals in separate staff dining facilities because it provides a break from direct inmate-related duties and contact. Unfortunately, this dining practice has a negative effect on the overall correctional environment. When staff and inmates eat the same food, prepared with the

same equipment, but eat in separate rooms, there is a perception by inmates that their food is or may be substandard. While the perception may be distorted, it contributes to the we/they dichotomy characteristic of many correctional institutions. To the extent possible, elimination of a we/they attitude on the part of both staff and inmates is probably the most significant and effective way to improve an institutional environment.

A good place to begin is in the dining room by providing a single dining area for both staff and inmates. Success in eliminating barriers in the dining room will improve the institution's chances of success elsewhere and will make highly visible the administration's basic philosophy and attitude concerning the inmates.

Because the dining room is the most frequently used service facility in the institution, its location is a key institutional design element. The main entrance to the dining room should be near the main inmate circulation routes, and entrances and exits should be separated to minimize cross-traffic.

Dining Room. The dining room should be large enough to seat from 45 to 50 percent of the total inmate population and 10 percent of the staff at any one time. For a facility of 500 inmates, this translates to about 4,000 square feet, which also allows sufficient space for official visitors. While permitting inmates to go to the dining room anytime during established eating periods is generally good for morale, some institutions control the

traffic by assigning inmates to designated shifts.

The dining room should be an attractive, pleasant, informal setting. Seating at four- to six-person tables in a colorful room designed to reduce noise levels encourages a relaxed atmosphere and reduces institutional regimentation and tensions. Moveable furniture allows flexibility in the use of the space and has proved very satisfactory in many institutions. The fixed, virtually indestructible pedestal-type table made of stainless steel is not only expensive but usually not necessary except, perhaps, in the most maximum security facilities.

The dining room is inappropriate space for other activities, such as movies, because of the time required for dining and cleaning up and the necessity of maintaining good sanitation.

Serving Lines. Food is almost always served cafeteria style. Inmates should enter the dining room and proceed to the serving lines that abut the food preparation area. Both the serving lines and the area planned for waiting lines should be arranged so there is minimal interference with those who are eating. If the facility is

Many facilities use a common dining room for both staff and inmates to break down the traditional "we/they" dichotomy and make visible the administration's positive attitude toward inmates (opposite). The dining room should be an attractive, pleasant, informal setting. Seating at four- to six-person tables (left) in a colorful room designed to reduce noise levels encourages a relaxed atmosphere and reduces institutional regimentation and tensions.

not located in a temperate climate, a sufficient indoor waiting area should be planned. Outdoor waiting areas should be sheltered from the elements.

The serving lines each require about 250 square feet and should be located between the dining room and the food preparation area. Two serving lines are needed to serve meals to a population of 500 in a reasonable period of time; one line is normally sufficient for less than 400 inmates. The two lines should be identical and should include griddles (with ventilation) for preparation of foods such as eggs. The wall between each serving line and the food preparation area should be equipped with heated, refrigerated, and room temperature pass-through cabinets for holding food until it is needed.

Beverage Stations. Hot and cold drinks are dispensed at beverage stations, each requiring about 25 square feet. Although the number of stations needed depends on the configuration of the dining space, one or two stations are usually sufficient. Cups, glasses, ice, water, and all prepared beverages should be available at each station. Condiments and salads are sometimes served adjacent to the stations. The beverage stations should be close to, but not part of, the serving lines, thus enabling diners to obtain refills without going through the lines.

Food Preparation

The preparation of food can vary from pre-plated frozen meals to full in-house preparation, including meat butchering. While the type of food service provided by airlines has proved very satisfactory for small facilities where inmates stay only a short time, this service is not recommended for long-term confinement. It is important to retain a professional food service consultant to advise the facility's planners about the latest food preparation techniques, equipment, and organizational designs. The choice of food preparation techniques will determine not only the size and organization of the kitchen, but also equipment needs, staff requirements, and capital and operating costs. Some facilities may be required to provide a separate area for preparing special foods, such as kosher food. Planners should assess the need for such special requirements before engaging a food service consultant.

The discussion below assumes that the facility's food service program will not engage in complete food preparation, which would in-

The type of food service program planned for the facility will greatly affect the amount of space, staff, and equipment required. However, since inmates typically comprise a large portion of the workforce, more space is required than would be necessary in a commercial kitchen.

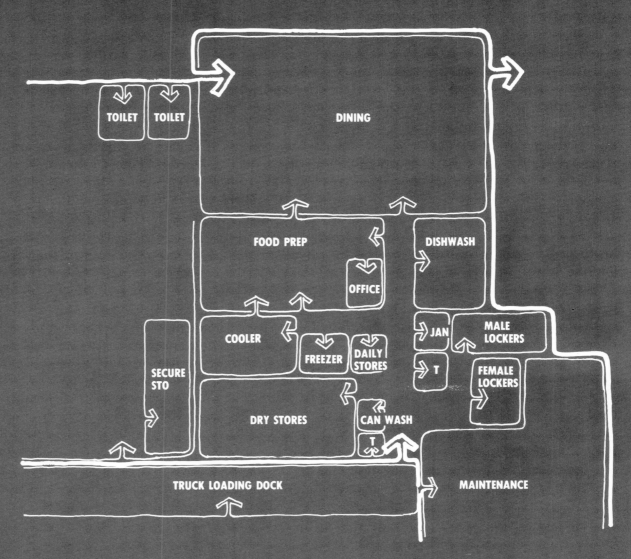

FOOD SERVICE

clude meat processing, or use only pre-plated foods. Rather, the guidelines are designed for a more typical program that involves the use of some pre-portioned items, preparation of fresh and frozen meats and vegetables, and a small in-house bakery.

Food Preparation Area. The food preparation area should be adjacent to the dining room. Specific areas should be designated for preparing vegetables, salads, meats, and pastries. If the dining dishes are washed in a separate room, the food preparation area requires about 1,200 square feet; if tray carts are used, approximately 1,500 square feet are needed (see "Dishwashing Area" below). These square footage recommendations assume that inmates compose a principal portion of the workforce. As a consequence, more space is required than in a commercial kitchen.

Planners may decide to operate a vocational training program in food service. If the program is small, there probably will be no design implications for the food preparation area. A large training program, however, may require larger areas and additional spaces, such as classrooms or offices.

Food Service Office. An office of about 200 square feet should be provided for the food service administrator and support staff. It should be placed so that it affords good surveillance of the food preparation area. Window walls should be used to facilitate supervision.

Storage Space

The food service function requires ample space for storage of supplies and materials. For easy handling of deliveries, all storage rooms should be on the same level as the truck dock.

Daily Supply Storage. Approximately 100 square feet should be provided for storing the food supplies

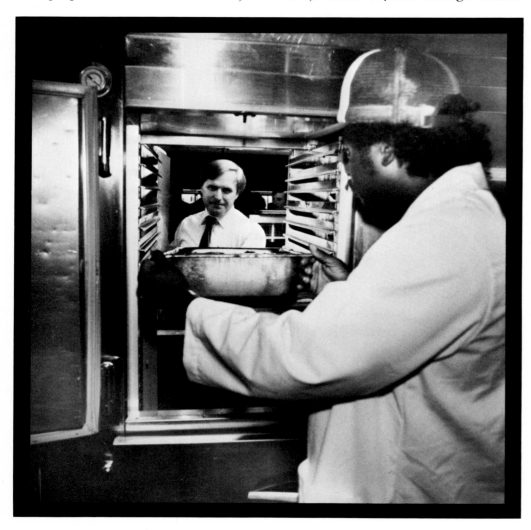

The wall between the serving lines and the food preparation area should be equipped with heated, refrigerated, and room temperature pass-through cabinets for holding food until it is needed.

needed for each day's meals. This area should be immediately accessible to the food preparation area, thereby diminishing the need for frequent trips to the main dry food storage area.

Dry Food Storage. A dry storage room, generally about 1,600 square feet, is needed for storing all foods and staple ingredients that do not require refrigeration. This area, which is distinct from the institution's warehouse, should be directly accessible to the truck dock and adjacent to the food preparation area.

Cool Storage. A cool storage room of about 600 square feet should be provided adjacent to the food preparation area for storing all dairy products, meats, vegetables, fruits, beverages, and prepared and unprepared foods that require chilling. This area is sometimes subdivided into separate units with individual entrances to allow different foods to be stored at various temperatures.

Freezer Storage. A 500-square-foot freezer room adjacent to the food preparation area is needed for storing prepared and unprepared foods that require subfreezing temperatures.

Dishwashing Area

There are two basic methods of cleaning dishes, utensils, and trays. The first provides two separate areas for washing dining dishes and food preparation utensils; the second combines the two dishwashing functions in one space.

Drop-off Window/Dishwashing Area. Facilities using this method provide a dishwashing room and drop-off window near the dining room exit. This minimizes worker time by having diners bring their own trays directly to the dishwashing area. The drop-off-window type of dishwashing room requires approximately 500 square feet. An additional area for washing food preparation utensils is located in the food preparation area; in this case, the food preparation area requires about 1,200 square feet.

Because the area for washing dishes is usually located adjacent to the dining room, designers must pay particular attention to suppressing the noise produced by the dishwashing equipment, as well as the odors and the unsightliness associated with such an area. Noise, for example, can be suppressed by a conveyor system and wall baffles. Otherwise, this solution will greatly detract from the overall atmosphere of the dining room.

There has been a tendency in the past to have the dishwashing activities open to view for surveillance from the dining room. While understandable, such an arrangement allows more counterproductive noise to spill into the dining room. If managers insist on open views of the dishwashing room, multiple-layer glass partitions should be used.

Combination Dishwashing Area. The second, and preferred, method of handling trays and dining dishes is to provide several tray carts along exit paths in the dining room where diners deposit their trays. Each tray cart requires about 20 square feet; four carts are usually sufficient. Food service workers transport the carts to a dishwashing room in the food preparation area where both dining dishes and food preparation utensils are washed. This system confines the utensil/dishwashing function to, or near, the food preparation area and limits the transmission of noise and odors to the dining room.

Except for special housing programs such as the medical and segregation units, a single, central dining area is preferable to either separate dining facilities in each housing unit or inmates taking their meals in their rooms. Inmates look forward to meals as a social time, which group dining enhances, and as a break from the routine of institutionalized living.

Locating the entire dishwashing function in the food preparation area means that the food preparation area should be about 1,500 square feet.

Additional Areas

Can Washing Area. If an institution cannot dispose of all food wastes by a garbage disposal system, a can washing area is needed, usually located in an outside alcove on or near the truck dock at the rear of the food preparation area. A special device is available for cleaning and sanitizing the food scrap cans quickly and easily.

Lockers and Toilets. The inmates and staff who work in the kitchen are usually provided with separate locker rooms equipped with toilets. The locker rooms should be near the food preparation area and, depending on the size of the inmate and staff workforce, will vary from approximately 100 to 175 square feet. Two staff locker rooms will be needed if female staff are employed in this area.

Janitor's Closet. A closet for cleaning materials and implements should be located adjacent to the food preparation area.

The preferred method of handling dish washing is to provide an area where both dining dishes and food preparation utensils are washed. This alternative reduces the transmission of noise and odors to the dining room.

The canteen, or commissary, offers for sale items that are not routinely issued to inmates by the institution, such as cigarettes, candy, ice cream, cookies, soap, deodorant, fruit, soda, greeting cards, radios, and shaving supplies. The canteen may be open seven days a week, often during evening hours so as not to interfere with inmate work schedules. While most inmates should be able to go to the central canteen for their purchases, an order form is usually used for inmates in segregation or other special units.

The accounting system used and associated equipment will determine the size of the space needed for this operation. Planners are advised to research this issue with the business staff or other appropriate staff.

The business office typically administers the canteen operation. A supervisor and a full-time assistant, assisted by carefully selected inmates, are usually needed to operate a canteen at a facility for 500 inmates. In addition, the security staff often provide staff support during sales periods.

The canteen comprises a sales and waiting area, an office, and a storage

CANTEEN

room. Since this service is used regularly by the inmate population, it is best located on major inmate circulation paths. A one-way queuing system is often used to provide ease of access and control traffic. Because of the frequent deliveries of supplies, the canteen storage room should have easy access to the truck dock and rear sally port. The perimeter of the canteen must be securely constructed. (See the section in Chapter IX on security construction.)

Waiting Line. To organize the traffic flow, the canteen should be designed with two doors, one for entering and one for exiting. An area of approximately 200 square feet should be provided inside the entrance where a line can form leading to the sales counter; this will accommodate about 20 inmates atany one time. A display area showing the items available should be located so that inmates can decide on their purchases while waiting in line.

Sales Area. The waiting line should proceed to a sales area of approximately 150 square feet, equipped with a sales counter and shelving behind the counter for stocking sales items. A cooler and freezer are recommended for storing the day's supplies of chilled and frozen items; to economize space, this equipment can be located under the counter. The counter should be long enough to accommodate two to three people working simultaneously. To prevent theft or unauthorized distribution of items over the counter, a transparent barrier with a pass-through window is often erected over the counter.

The canteen may be open seven days a week, often during evening hours so as not to interfere with inmate work schedules. While most inmates should be able to go to the central canteen for their purchases, an order form is usually used for inmates in segregation or other special units.

Canteen Office.   An office of approximately 150 square feet will accommodate two staff members and the canteen's recordkeeping functions. The office should be situated so there is easy access to both the sales area and the storage room. It should also be accessible to people who need to conduct business with canteen staff when the sales counter is not open.

Storage Room.   A nearby storage room of about 800 square feet is needed for stocking sales items. About 1,200 linear feet of steel shelving is needed for storing certain items such as toiletries, although most items can be stacked on the floor on pallets. Freezer and cooler space should also be provided. The storage room should be easily accessible to the truck dock as well as the canteen office and sales area.

Toilet, Janitor's Closet.   This facility, located within the storage room, enables staff and inmate use while they are locked inside the canteen.

A display cabinet helps inmates decide on their purchases while waiting in line. A transparent barrier above the sales counter prevents theft or unauthorized distribution of merchandise over the counter.

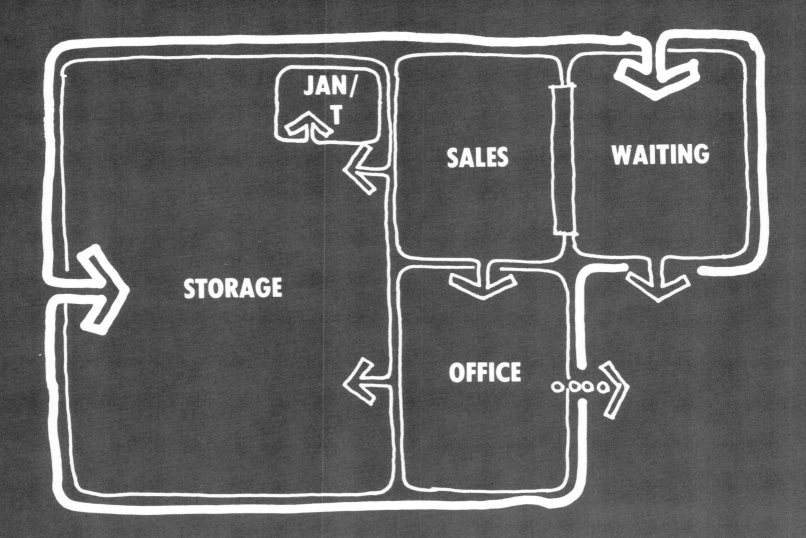

JAN/T

SALES

WAITING

STORAGE

OFFICE

CANTEEN

The importance of correspondence between relatives and friends becomes greatly magnified in a correctional setting. Frequent visiting by inmates' families is not always feasible because of such factors as financial constraints and location. Thus correspondence should be encouraged between inmates and their families, friends, and other associates to maintain ties with the outside. Moreover, correspondence between inmates and their attorneys and the courts must be assured. This usually requires special handling, adding to the complexities of the mail operation.

The mail room is the area through which all incoming and outgoing mail passes. Although processing outgoing mail is an important function, the mail room staff's primary task is opening, inspecting, and sorting incoming inmate mail. There are usually comprehensive rules and regulations governing correspondence, based on the need to maintain security. The control of contraband entering the institution is a major concern—unless incoming inmate mail is opened and inspected, the staff lose control of contraband entering

MAIL ROOM

through the mail.

Legal mail and other privileged correspondence usually require special handling. Such mail must be recorded and frequently must be opened in the mail room in the presence of the inmate. Catalog orders by inmates also require special handling.

Outgoing inmate mail is not usually inspected. Inmates generally drop outgoing mail in a box in their housing unit, where it is collected daily and brought to the mail room.

If possible, administrative mail should be kept separate from inmate

mail. This can usually be arranged with the postal authorities. Staff members should be assigned individual locked mailed boxes.

The mail room requires at least one full-time staff member, with regular clerical support and part-time assistance during holidays when the volume of correspondence is high. As a rule, the mail room staff are a part of the security staff. Increasingly, however, they are placed under the supervision of the business office. Inmates should be absolutely prohibited from working in the mail room.

The size of the mail room in a 500-capacity correctional facility will vary according to the complexity and diversity of operations assigned to this area. It should typically contain about 150 square feet, although some jurisdictions may require a larger space. While off-limits to the inmate population, the mail room should be located near major staff traffic patterns so staff members can pick up their mail daily. It should also be near the cashier's office because money sent to inmates must be given to the cashier to credit to their accounts. Because there are considerable limita-

Although processing outgoing mail is an important function, the mail room staff's primary task is opening, inspecting, and sorting incoming inmate mail. . . . The control of contraband entering the institution is a major concern—unless incoming inmate mail is opened and inspected, the staff lose control of contraband entering through the mail.

tions on the amount of personal property an inmate may keep during confinement, it is recommended that the mail room also be located near the admissions and discharge area to facilitate the mailing of prohibited personal property to inmates' relatives and friends.

Sufficient space must be provided for mail processing equipment and temporary storage of letters, packages, magazines, and newspapers. A locked cabinet is needed to store inmates' mail that occasionally is rejected for delivery. In addition, because some mail must be opened in the presence of an inmate, a special area must be designed to separate the inmate from the general mail processing area.

Finally, because the control of contraband is one of the major responsibilities of mailroom staff, the room must be constructed with secure walls, doors, and windows to prevent inmates from entering without authorization.

Individual staff mail boxes should be located on a main staff circulation route. Inmates should never be allowed to work in the mail room.

Laundry and Clothing Exchange

Facility planners should conduct a cost-benefit assessment to decide whether it is best to operate an in-house laundry or provide services through an outside contract. If an in-house service is provided, all laundry is usually done in a central facility, although some institutions provide small commercial-quality washers and dryers in the housing units for personal clothing.

The institutional laundry is customarily responsible for the procurement, laundering, storage, and distribution of all inmate clothing and institutional linens. Inmates usually bring their used clothing to the laundry to exchange for fresh sets of clothing; linens typically are exchanged in the housing unit and transported by carts or trucks.

The laundry is usually staffed by one full-time supervisor and one full-time assistant, with additional assistance provided by inmates. The clothing-issue operation generally does not require a full-time staff position.

Depending on local policy, space may be needed for dry-cleaning staff uniforms. It is recommended, how-

PERSONAL CARE SERVICES

ever, that dry cleaning not be done at the institution. The machinery is expensive to purchase and maintain, consumes additional space, and requires additional staff time to operate. Moreover, some dry cleaning chemicals are considered carcinogenic and are subject to strict government regulations that require expensive equipment. The need for dry cleaning is also diminishing because of the increasing use of wash-and-wear fabrics for uniforms.

The laundry area must include space for the short-term storage and exchange of clothing and linens, ideally in close proximity to the laundry machines. In addition, space for

mending and long-term storage should be provided.

The laundry should be near major inmate circulation paths so inmates can easily exchange their clothing. It should also have direct access to the truck loading dock to receive deliveries.

Laundry Room. The size of the laundry room, as well as the size and type of laundry equipment needed, depends on the types of fabric to be laundered, the amount of laundry, and the frequently of laundering. Facility planners should engage a professional laundry consultant to determine the most suitable equipment for the institution. If, for example, the institution uses mostly wash-and-wear clothing and cotton bedding and towels, and provides three clothing changes per week, the facility would need one 250-pound washer, one 100-pound washer, three 100-pound dryers, and various pressers. This equipment could be accommodated in a room of about 1,000 square feet. The precise square footage needed, however, will fluctuate with the equipment selected.

Clothing Exchange. Clothing

The preferred, and more personal, method of exchanging clothing is to store and issue clothing by name so that the inmate receives the same set of clothes each time.

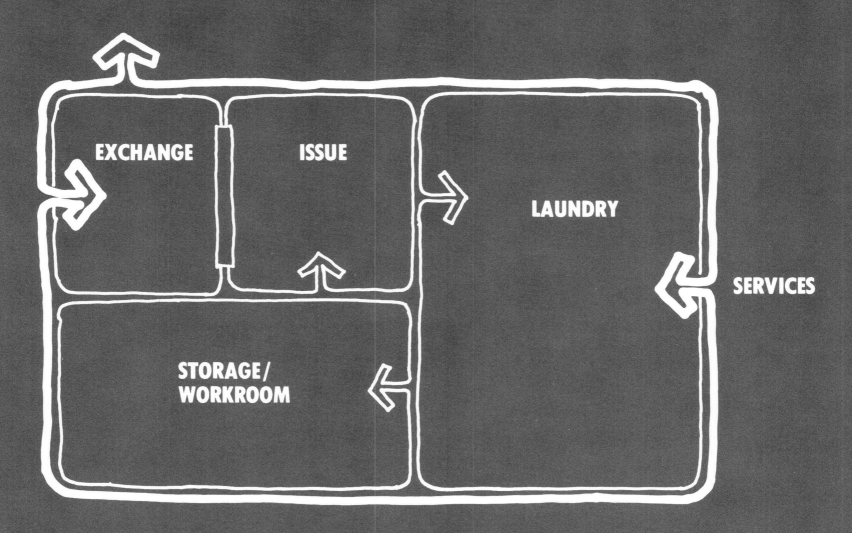

EXCHANGE

ISSUE

LAUNDRY

SERVICES

STORAGE/
WORKROOM

LAUNDRY and
CLOTHING EXCHANGE

Some facilities operate central laundries where all inmate clothing and linens are laundered. Equipment needed will depend on the volume, type and composition of the articles to be laundered.

exchanges are handled in two basic ways, each of which affects the space required for this operation. Regardless of the method chosen, the clothing exchange area should be located adjacent to the laundry room and should contain a lobby area of approximately 120 square feet. Both methods also require storage shelving or bins.

The preferred, and more personal, method of exchanging clothing is to store and issue clothing by name so that the inmate receives the same sets of clothes each time. This method requires about 800 to 1,000 square feet to accommodate shelving or bins for sorting by individual name.

The less preferable, and less personal, method is to store and issue clothing by size. Although this method requires less sorting time and less space—an area of 600 square feet is usually sufficient—it produces a negative effect on the correctional environment and contributes to the we/they dichotomy discussed earlier.

Storage/Workroom. A separate room of approximately 750 square feet should be provided adjacent to the clothing exchange or laundry room for storing off-season clothing and extra supplies of linen and clothing. In addition, folding, sorting, and mending can be performed here.

If shoes are repaired at the institution, this room is a logical location for this activity but should contain an additional 200 square feet.

Hair Care Service

Although a barber or hair styling service is sometimes located in each major housing area, a centralized hair care function will generally provide better services, contribute to a more normal environment, and offer an opportunity for formal hair care training that will be useful to inmates after their release. Special arrangements may be needed for providing hair care to patients in the medical or segregation units if their stay in these units is prolonged.

Most hair care services are performed by inmates who already have barber skills or have received training while at the institution. A staff member usually supervises this area.

Central Hair Care Shop. The shop should be located on one of the major inmate circulation paths. A single room of 400 to 500 square feet should adequately serve this function. Two or three stations with barber chairs, hair-washing sinks, and storage cabinets should be provided.

Other institutions place small commercial-quality washers and dryers in housing units for personal clothing. This technique provides an opportunity for inmates to assume a major responsibility for their own care.

4
INMATE
PROGRAMS

Once they have been formally admitted to a facility, inmates should participate in an orientation program. The purpose of orientation is to introduce the inmate to the facility in an orderly fashion and to make the transition to institutional life as smooth as possible. An orientation program generally includes lectures, handouts, and films that explain the facility's mission, programs, rules, regulations, and staff expectations of inmates. At the same time, the program gives staff an opportunity to learn as much as they can about the new inmate. Each new inmate receives a comprehensive medical exam, and staff administer tests and conduct in-depth interviews to help determine the best program and work assignments for the inmate.

Some jurisdictions dedicate an entire facility to the purpose of orientation and assessment. After sentencing, all inmates in these jurisdictions are sent to a reception facility where they are tested, interviewed, and given information about the facility where they will actually serve their sentence. These final assignments are based on the assessments conducted

ORIENTATION

at the reception facility. This guide does not address the design of a reception facility, but rather explores the basic options—and design implications—for operating an orientation program at each individual facility.

There are basically three options for housing inmates during their orientation. The first is to provide a special orientation housing unit adjacent to the admissions area. The second is to designate all or part of a regular housing unit for newly admitted inmates. The third basic option is to provide no special housing at all but simply assign inmates to units as beds become available.

The first option, which requires a separate housing unit near the admissions function, is the only one of the three with design and construction implications. One reason for providing separate housing is to keep new inmates apart from the general population as much as possible. Newly admitted inmates are escorted to the main dining room for meals as well as to the visiting room, medical facility, and gym. This alternative may be used when staff lack adequate information about the inmate upon admission to make a permanent unit assignment. This is particularly important where units have specific missions or house only one type of inmate, such as predators or potential victims. The number of rooms in a separate orientation unit is determined by the number of new admissions anticipated at any one time and the length of the orientation program. It is unlikely that this unit will be as large as a regular housing unit, although the physical requirements will be similar to those for

The purpose of orientation is to introduce the inmate to the facility in an orderly fashion and to make the transition to institutional life as smooth as possible.

general housing, including single-occupancy rooms of 60 to 80 square feet and space for staff offices and leisure activities. Since the program is conducted in an independent housing unit, additional staff are required.

The second option dedicates an entire housing module or part of a module for orientation housing. As with the first option, it is assumed that staff do not have sufficient information to assign newly admitted inmates to their permanent units. If the facility wishes to separate new inmates from the general population, the entire module of 40 to 65 rooms should be designated as orientation housing. It is unlikely, though, that the number of inmates in orientation at any one time will match the number of beds in a module. If separation from the general population is not a major concern, a part of the module can be used for orientation housing. While this practice places new inmates with the general population, it permits greater flexibility in adjusting the number of beds available for orientation and makes more efficient use of available space.

Under the third option, staff assign inmates to their permanent housing unit immediately following admission. No special construction or additional staff are required and beds are utilized efficiently. This approach assumes that the staff have sufficient data from the courts, pre-sentence investigation reports, and other sources to make an informed decision about where each inmate should be assigned—whether, for example, to a unit for aggressive inmates, or to a unit for drug abusers. Once the assignment has been made, the inmate participates in the regular orientation program and staff begin to assess in more detail the program and work assignments most appropriate for each new inmate.

Orientation is a time for staff to learn as much as they can about the new inmate. This will facilitate housing placement, and program or work assignment.

VISITING

A sound visitation program is essential to the successful operation of any correctional institution. Frequent visits by family members and friends help maintain family and community ties, lessen the negative psychological consequences of confinement, and implant attitudes that are important for successful reentry into the community following confinement. In addition, visitation strengthens inmate morale and contributes to an easing of tensions and management problems. Visitors include lawyers, parole advisors who assist in release planning, and members of the clergy who may provide counseling to help resolve family problems.

In recognition of these issues, the courts have consistently upheld the right of inmates to receive visitors while granting wide discretion to correctional administrators as to how the visitation programs should be conducted. There are, however, certain features or practices that should be an integral part of every program.

As a general policy, contact visiting is preferred. In addition, visiting hours should not be overly restrictive. At a minimum, the chief executive officer should permit visiting on Saturdays, Sundays, and holidays. Because restrictions may be a hardship to some families and other visitors, more generous, flexible visiting hours are strongly encouraged in order to maximize visiting opportunities, as are exceptions to accommodate off-hour visiting for those unable to schedule their visits during the institution's regular visiting hours.

The number of visitors an inmate may receive and the length of visits should be limited only by the institution's schedule, space, and personnel constraints or by other substantive reasons that justify limitations.

Because family members are the most frequent visitors, the institution's policy should permit visits by children. Allowing visits by children further strengthens family ties, which can be strained during confinement, and reduces any child-care problems associated with visits. This practice can make visiting more frequent and convenient and less expensive.

Visitors should be received in a waiting room or lobby area that conveys a hospitable, non-threatening atmosphere. Their arrival should be recorded, identities checked, and the inmate notified of their arrival. Provision must be made to store visitors' personal belongings that are prohibited inside the institution. Body searches of inmates are often conducted both before and after visits to ensure that no contraband has been passed during the visit.

Private rooms are needed for visits with attorneys to permit the free exchange of information and documents necessary in privileged communications between attorneys and their clients. These areas can also

As a general policy, contact visiting is preferred. In addition, visiting hours should not be overly restrictive. At a minimum, the chief executive officer should permit visiting on Saturdays, Sundays, and holidays.

serve as secure visiting rooms for inmates who present serious escape risks or whose behavior may be disruptive.

Visiting programs are usually supervised by two or three full-time members of the security staff. While staff supervision is mandatory, it should be carried out in the least intrusive manner possible. Although some can be provided by moving about the visiting room, there should also be a staff station in the visiting room that affords good visibility of the entire area. Surveillance of the visiting room should not be carried out solely through the use of closed circuit television or audio monitors.

Some visits require special arrangements. For example, visitors to inmates in segregation units or the infirmary can be escorted to these areas where the visits can be held in individual rooms or in existing multiuse space. In the case of inmates in segregation, the administration may also choose to use the private visiting rooms in the main visiting room. Whatever arrangements are made, these visits should be supervised.

All visitors should enter the institution through the front pedestrian

Mirrored glass has been used in some visiting rooms to create a bright attractive space (above), while enhancing the privacy of the visitors (below).

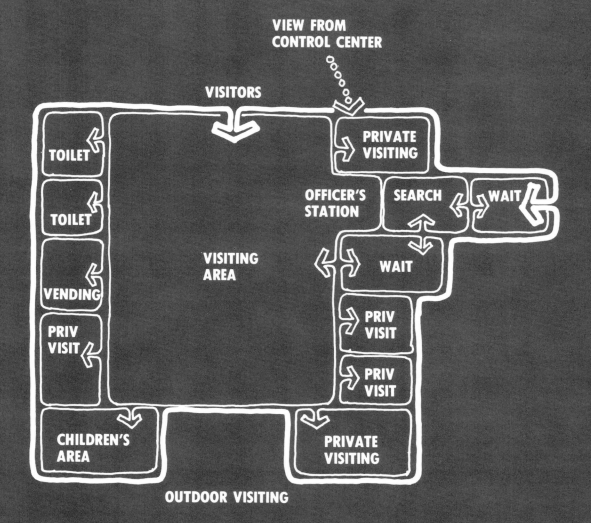

VIEW FROM
CONTROL CENTER

VISITORS

PRIVATE
VISITING

TOILET

TOILET

OFFICER'S
STATION

SEARCH

WAIT

VISITING
AREA

VENDING

WAIT

PRIV
VISIT

PRIV
VISIT

PRIV
VISIT

CHILDREN'S
AREA

PRIVATE
VISITING

OUTDOOR VISITING

VISITING

The visiting room should be designed as pleasant, informal, multi-purpose space that can be used for other activities. The design should promote communication and place no barriers between inmates or visitors and staff. Seating arrangements, color schemes, and textures should convey a residential character.

entrance where a receptionist is stationed on the outer side of the sally port. Visitors should be screened by metal detectors, and packages being brought into the visiting room should be inspected. In addition to a waiting area, lockers should be available to store visitors' hats, coats, and other belongings that cannot be taken into the visiting room. Telephones for public use should be located in the waiting area. Frequently, space is provided for the display and sale of craft items made by the inmates.

Visitors must pass through the sally port and proceed directly to the visiting room. Locating the visiting area near the front sally port diminishes traffic to other areas of the institution and prevents unauthorized visitor contact with inmates.

Visiting Room. In general, the size of the visiting room is determined by the projected number of inmates receiving visitors and the average number of visitors at any one time during the visiting period. One of the most difficult problems in designing the room is arriving at an accurate estimate of the number of visitors to be accommodated. The number of inmates visiting at any one time will depend on the number of visiting hours established by the institution. If there are generous daily visiting hours, fewer inmates will be visiting at a single time and less space will be required. Experience has shown that a typical visiting room for an institution for 500 inmates should accommodate a minimum of 150 people and have at least 2,000 square feet of space.

The visiting room should be located so that minimal supervision of visitor traffic is needed. The most efficient way to supervise visitor traffic is by placing the control center, discussed in Chapter VII, along the path between the sally port and the visiting room, thus eliminating the need for additional supervisory staff along this route. Distinctly separate entrances to the visiting room for visitors and inmates must be maintained. A correctional officer should be located in the visiting room for general supervision. The officer should also ensure that no inmates leave through the visitor's entrance.

The visiting area should be designed as a pleasant, informal, multi-purpose space that can be converted to other uses consistent with the goals of the visiting program (group meetings, counseling sessions, etc.). The design should promote informal communication and place no architectural barriers between inmates and visitors or inmates and staff. Seating arrangements, color schemes, and textures should convey a residential character.

To encourage inmates and their visitors to communicate freely and in confidence, efforts should be made to ensure at least a small amount of privacy. Aural and visual privacy can be enhanced by using furniture to form low dividers separating the visiting area into zones, although the dividers should not jeopardize supervision of the area. In addition, efforts should be made to minimize sounds coming from other areas of the institution.

Private Visiting Rooms. Several private visiting rooms should be provided in the visiting area to serve individual inmates and their visitors, including lawyers, clergy, parole advisors, and, in some jurisdictions, private family visits. The rooms should accommodate different numbers of visitors: one should be large enough to accommodate about six people, and the others, all of equal size, should accommodate up to four.

Decisionmakers are urged to provide most inmates with "contact" visiting facilities. One or two non-contact visiting rooms are often included in the design, visible from other areas of the visiting room and, if possible, from the control center. This facilitates the task of staff surveillance, particularly during off-hour visiting when a correctional officer may not be available for assignment to the visiting room.

Search Room. A private room for contraband searches should be located at the inmate's entrance/exit to the visiting area. The room should contain about 120 square feet and include toilet facilities. It should also ensure some privacy from other inmates as well as visitors.

Children's Area. Approximately 300 square feet of space adjacent to the visiting room should be provided to accommodate small children. Play equipment should be available and the area should be supervised. This facility is often constructed by inmate

An outdoor visiting space provides a pleasant, natural environment for visiting. Play areas for children should also be incorporated.

labor after the institution has opened.

Vending Area. An area of approximately 150 square feet should be located adjacent to the visiting room for vending machines dispensing coffee, soft drinks, candy, and, perhaps, cigarettes and sandwiches or other snacks. The area frequently includes a snack bar. An adjacent 50-square-foot storage room is recommended. It is desirable to place the vending machines behind a screen or partition, but the area must remain visible from the officer's station in the visiting room.

Visitors' Toilets. Separate men's and women's toilet facilities, each with 150 square feet, should be provided for visitors to minimize the potential for passing of contraband and to ensure privacy. Both should be equipped with fixtures suitable for handicapped persons.

Outside Visiting Area. An outdoor visiting area within the secure perimeter of the facility is highly recommended. In favorable weather, this provides a pleasant, natural environment for visiting; on busy days, it provides overflow space. A play area for children can also be included along with play equipment. An additional outdoor area located outside the secure perimeter can be used for inmates requiring minimal supervision. Outdoor visiting areas must offer access to toilet facilities and other indoor visitors' services. Shade and rain shelters may also be appropriate in certain climates.

Vending facilities with snacks and drinks should be available for visitors. This area should be visible from the officers' station.

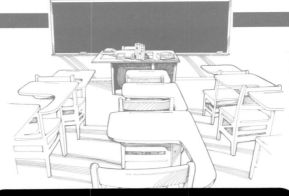

EDUCATION

Educational programs often assume special importance in correctional facilities. Many inmates' educational backgrounds are seriously deficient. Numerous inmates lack a high school diploma, while many others have less than a sixth-grade education. A sound education program should provide a well-rounded general education. It should offer a variety of programs including: an Adult Basic Education (ABE) program for inmates who have not attained a sixth-grade education; a General Education Development (GED) program so that inmates can work toward their high school equivalency; a post-secondary education program for those who have successfully completed high school and want to further their education; and continuing education courses for those who want to update their skills and knowledge.

The education program not only provides inmates with a constructive way to spend time, it also gives many the opportunity to improve their skills and thus better their chances of finding employment after release. These programs also contribute to improving inmates' attitudes and self-esteem, again enhancing their chances of a successful adjustment to the community after release.

The education program area serves many functions other than academic education. It can be used for vocational training instruction, meetings, staff functions, as well as volunteer and other inmate activities. Consequently, it should be readily accessible to other programs or services.

Staff usually consist of a full-time program administrator, assistant, and clerk, as well as instructors specializing in ABE, GED, college level courses, and continuing education programs. Frequently, the full-time education staff are supplemented by contract staff who enrich the standard programs and offer special courses as the need arises.

Education programs should have two libraries for inmates—a general library and a legal library. The general library functions as a learning center and, from a design standpoint, becomes the nucleus of the education department. It should be similar to the library in a public education facility and have available a wide variety of books, periodicals, newspapers, and reference materials, as well as audiovisual materials for educational and recreational purposes. In addition, it should provide self-instructional materials to supplement regular classroom activities. Library materials must be kept relevant to the inmates' needs, and should reflect a variety of languages, if appropriate, as well as varied reading levels and interests. Usually, one staff member oversees the library, assisted by carefully selected inmates.

The general library frequently contains study carrels arranged so as to offer some degree of privacy.

The education program not only provides inmates with a constructive way to spend time, it also gives many the opportunity to improve their skills and thus better their chances of finding employment after release. These programs also contribute to improving inmates' attitudes and self-esteem, again enhancing their chances of a successful adjustment to the community after release.

Another approach to private study space is to set aside a classroom for this purpose. In either case, special provisions for electronic wiring are necessary for using audiovisual materials.

Access to legal materials by all inmates has been supported vigorously by the courts. The institution should ensure that inmates have access to the legal library seven days a week, particularly during evenings and weekends when work and school hours do not conflict with library hours. Normally, the staff who oversee the general library also oversee the legal library. The American Association of Law Libraries has developed lists of titles of materials appropriate for legal

reference libraries, and these lists have become a standard by which courts have measured the adequacy of inmate law libraries. The lists include such materials as state constitutions and statutes, state court cases, federal case law, court rules and practices, as well as legal periodicals, digests, and indexes. Many of the required materials are available on microfilm.

Classrooms.   It is recommended that a variety of classrooms be provided to accommodate different class sizes and enhance their adaptability for other activities. Two rooms of approximately 500 square feet each, two smaller rooms of about 350 square feet each, and one room of

about 800 square feet are suggested. The precise number and size of classrooms will vary depending on the educational needs of the inmate population and the other training programs provided at the facility.

Designers should follow the accepted standards for designing classrooms in public educational facilities. No security features are needed except, perhaps, in maximum security institutions.

Video Classroom.   A specialized soundproof room designed for videotaping is recommended. This 500-square-foot space should contain conduits to hold wiring for lighting, microphones, video recorders, and other audiovisual items. The room can also be used as a regular classroom when needed.

Media Preparation Room.   It is advisable to provide a small space of approximately 150 square feet for working on video programs and storing equipment and supplies, such as tape-duplicating equipment, cameras, tripods, and lights. This space should be adjacent to the video classroom.

Staff Offices.   Approximately five staff offices are required, including a supervisor's office with about

Education is one of the most important programs offered in a correctional facility. For many inmates, the personal attention provided by the staff helps them gain the educational skills that are crucial to their success in the community.

Carrels in the education area offer some privacy for individual study.

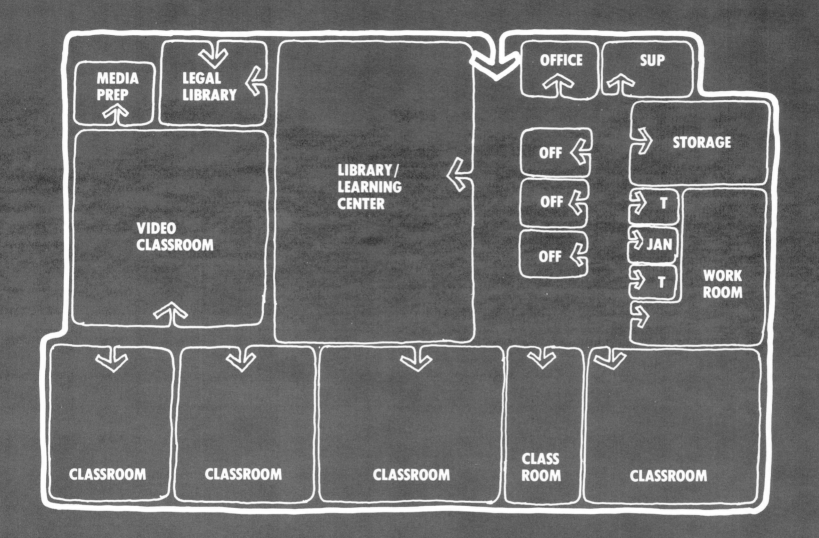

EDUCATIONAL

120 square feet, and four teachers' offices with 100 square feet each. In addition, a room with 250 square feet should be provided for a clerk, teachers' aides, and records storage. These offices usually are grouped together.

Storage/Workroom. This area should be about 200 square feet, providing room for such items as a worktable and a copy machine, and storage space for instructional materials.

Toilets. There should be separate toilets provided for staff and inmates in the education department.

General Library. The library functions as a learning center and is located so that it is the focal point of the education program. It should contain about 1,500 square feet, which provides sufficient space for a librarian's station, study carrels, leisure reading, self-instructional materials and equipment, and book stacks. The stacks should be arranged so that they do not create unnecessary blind spots and impede supervision.

The library should be equipped with sound-absorbing material such as carpeting, acoustic ceiling material, and upholstered furniture.

Storage Room. An area of approximately 200 square feet located adjacent to the library is usually adequate for storage.

Legal Library. The legal library is a component of the general library, but, if possible, should also be directly accessible from outside the education department so that inmates can still use the facility when the academic area is closed. A 200-square-foot area will accommodate about six people at one time and allow sufficient space for legal stacks, tables, chairs, typewriters, a photocopy machine, and microfilm viewers. Like the general library, it is important that this room include sound-absorbing materials.

Two libraries should be available to inmates—a general and a legal library. The general library should have a wide variety of books, periodicals, newspapers, reference materials, and audiovisual resources. The collection should be consistent with inmates' reading abilities, interests, and language preferences.

The primary goal of vocational training is to provide inmates with marketable skills so they are better equipped to earn a living for themselves and their dependents when released to the community. One of the critical issues faced by correctional administrators is designing the most appropriate vocational programs for teaching skills that will be highly marketable in the communities to which the inmates will return. Ideally, vocational programs should respond to the sometimes rapid changes occurring in the nation's job markets. The challenge for designers is to provide adequate and adaptable space that permits vocational programs to vary substantially over the life of the facility. In addition, investment in expensive, hard-to-move heavy equipment should be minimized because the use of such equipment tends to discourage timely program changes.

Traditional trades such as carpentry, plumbing, welding, painting, automotive repair, and electrical work are usually taught in the facility's maintenance shops and supplemented by classroom instruction (see Chapter VI, "Plant Maintenance Department"). The vocational train-

VOCATIONAL TRAINING

ing space is used to teach other trades such as computer programming, computer-related equipment operation and repair, and repairing small engines, office equipment, refrigerators, air conditioners, and televisions.

The vocational training program is usually supervised by the education department. The number of full-time instructors will vary according to the number of shop areas built into the design. If possible, however, it is recommended that three or four instructors with multiple skills be used to staff this program. Part-time con-

tract employees from a local vocational school can often be hired to augment the regular staff. The use of contract staff also allows greater flexibility when program modifications are needed in response to changes in the job market.

The vocational training space should be accessible by truck and located adjacent to the education department as well as the industrial program. This location offers the advantages of access to the academic classrooms for providing supplemental instruction and access to a loading dock to facilitate the delivery of equipment. Moreover, because programs change over the life of the facility, a location adjacent to the industrial program allows greater flexibility in converting industrial space to vocational space and vice versa as the need arises.

The design for this area must consider Occupational Safety and Health Administration (OSHA) standards as well as state and local safety standards regarding the storage of flammable liquids and ventilation of noxious fumes.

Vocational Shops. The vocational training area is generally a large, open space with approximately

The challenge for designers is to provide adequate and adaptable space that permits vocational programs to vary substantially over the life of the facility. . . . Since it is often difficult and perhaps inappropriate to identify specific programs during the early design stage, the vocational space should be constructed initially as a shell with a minimum clear ceiling height of 12 feet.

15,000 square feet, designed to be adaptable for a variety of activities. Since it is often difficult and perhaps inappropriate to identify specific programs during the early design stage, the vocational space should be constructed initially as a shell with a minimum clear ceiling height of 12 feet. During the construction period, when timely decisions are made about the types of programs to be provided, the most appropriate partitions can be planned. This approach will prevent costly alterations that otherwise might occur if program changes develop between the design and operational phases.

Adequate utilities should be distributed to the vocational training area, although provisions for the secondary distribution system should be made following the decisions on the specific programs to be provided. The required capacity is determined by estimating the range of vocational activities anticipated for the institution. Usually, little or no office space is needed in this area because staff can use offices in the adjacent academic area.

Toilets. Appropriate toilet facilities should be located near the entrance. A utility sink is desirable.

The primary goal of vocational training is to provide inmates with marketable skills. Ideally, vocational programs respond to the sometimes rapid changes in the nation's job markets.

A sound recreational program is a crucial element in any correctional facility. By providing inmates with constructive means for channeling energies and relieving the tensions inherent in institutional living, the program plays an important part in the safe and orderly operation of a facility. Recreational activities also give inmates an opportunity to use their free time constructively, improve their physical and mental health, develop good sportsmanship, and morale. Typically, the recreation program consists of a wide variety of organized group and individual activities, including various action sports, music, drama, movies, arts and crafts, and table games.

Ideally, at least two full-time recreation specialists should be available to coordinate the program, with assistance from security staff and carefully selected inmates. In addition, many community groups and individual volunteers contribute substantial time and effort to help coordinate programs and increase the variety of activities for the inmates. Both indoor and outdoor facilities are needed, as listed below.

RECREATION

Outdoor Recreation

Recreation Field. The outdoor recreation field should be located adjacent to the gymnasium so that participants are close to the toilets, showers, locker rooms, and equipment storage and issue area. An adjacent location also enables the recreation program staff to supervise gym and field activities more easily. A field of about five acres is recommended. This will provide sufficient space for several activities—baseball or softball, handball, volleyball, boccie, basketball, weight lifting, track—to take place at the same time. Courts should be hard-surfaced. Nighttime lighting and bleachers for spectators should also be provided.

Indoor Recreation

Gymnasium. An indoor gymnasium is highly desirable in any correctional institution used for long-term confinement. Even facilities in very temperate climates should provide at least an open-air shelter so that programs will not be curtailed during rainy weather.

Although the gymnasium and outdoor recreation field should be adjacent to one another, neither function should be located near the medical, segregation, or visiting facilities. This will prevent the noise from sports activities from impinging on the medical program and curtail opportunities for passing contraband.

A full-size regulation gymnasium

An indoor gymnasium is highly desirable in any correctional institution used for long-term confinement. Even facilities in very temperate climates should provide at least an open-air shelter so that programs will not be curtailed during rainy weather.

is recommended for formal competitive games, and to enable two half-court programs to be conducted simultaneously. Bleachers should be included for spectators. The total area required is about 7,500 square feet; the minimum ceiling height should be 22 feet.

Because the gymnasium is usually the only space large enough to accommodate the total inmate population at one time, the floor finish should be suitable for street-shoe traffic, portable chairs, and, perhaps, other furniture. A plasticized, poured floor covering is recommended rather than a floating wood floor, even though wood is a better surface for court games such as basketball. These provisions will allow the gym to be used for large gatherings such as concerts, plays, and meetings.

Chair Storage. Approximately 150 square feet of space should be available for stacked chair storage.

Weight Lifting. Weight lifting is a very popular program among inmates in most correctional institutions. It is recommended that a weight lifting room of about 500 square feet be located adjacent to both the gymnasium and the recreation supervisor's office so that staff can easily supervise this activity. The room should also be located on an outside wall, with direct access to the outdoors so that the program can be held outside during favorable weather. This feature makes the program available to a larger number of inmates. An outdoor court should be hard-surfaced.

Equipment Storage/Issue. This space should be located close to both the recreation field and the gymnasium so that it can serve both areas. It should contain about 350 square feet and be designed with one or two windows for issuing equipment.

The outdoor recreation space (above) provides inmates an opportunity to channel pent-up energies and relieve the tensions inherent in institutional living through vigorous physical activity. Weight lifting (below) is a popular activity in correctional facilities. This outdoor space is adjacent to an indoor weight room which is accessible through the double doors at the end of the building.

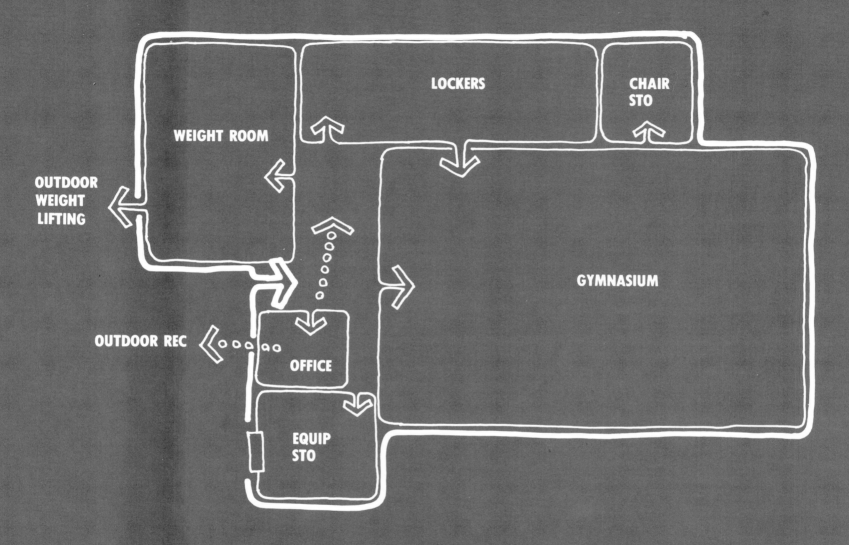

OUTDOOR
WEIGHT
LIFTING

WEIGHT ROOM

LOCKERS

CHAIR
STO

OUTDOOR REC

OFFICE

EQUIP
STO

GYMNASIUM

RECREATION

Toilets and Showers/Lockers. A space of approximately 250 square feet should be located so that it is accessible from both the gymnasium and the outside recreation field. The area should be equipped with about 25 lockers, three wash basins, two toilets, and four showers. A larger facility is usually unnecessary because inmates frequently use the toilets and showers in their housing units.

Supervisor's Office. The supervisor's office should be located near the gymnasium and recreation yard, with a good view of these two areas for supervision. Approximately 150 square feet provides adequate space for recordkeeping and storage of items requiring special care, such as a portable scoreboard and calibration equipment.

Recreation Room. A large indoor area of approximately 1,800 square feet should be equipped as a recreation room where inmates can play games and socialize. Activities such as billiards or pool, table tennis, shuffleboard, checkers, chess, and certain types of card games are usually planned for this area. Supervision generally is provided by the security staff.

Because this room is heavily used, it should be located along major inmate circulation paths. This room functions particularly well if it is located near the arts and crafts shop or multi-use rooms, areas also used for leisure activities and usually in use during the same time of day or evening. If the room is constructed with a good view of the area within the perimeter security, this not only reinforces the open atmosphere of the recreation facility, but also facilities casual supervision of this room from the outside. A small room with approximately 80 square feet should be located adjacent to the recreation room for storing equipment and materials.

Arts and Crafts Shop. Many institutional recreation programs provide arts and crafts activities, giving inmates an opportunity to use their spare time in a constructive and creative manner. Virtually all arts and crafts activities are suitable for a correctional facility. A qualified instructor, often engaged part-time through a contract, oversees this program.

The arts and crafts program is usually a popular activity and should be located near major inmate circulation paths, perhaps close to the multi-use areas or the academic area. A large room of about 1,200 square feet should be provided for this activity. Because this room requires large pieces of equipment that remain set up, it should not be considered for multi-use purposes. The room should have sufficient electrical service to operate a kiln and should contain two sinks equipped with plaster traps.

A secure storage room of about 150 square feet should be located adjacent to the arts and crafts shop. The room should contain shelving for work in progress and for supplies and materials. "Shadow boards" containing outlines of certain tools may be needed to ensure that all tools are returned.

A full-size gymnasium permits various activities to take place simultaneously such as volleyball, basketball, and handball.

Historically, religious programs have played a significant role in correctional facilities. The right of religious expression is a constitutional guarantee, and the courts have upheld vigorously the right of inmates to be given reasonable opportunities to pursue their religious beliefs during confinement. Thus, correctional facilities must offer flexible religious programs that will allow all inmates to exercise their religious beliefs.

The religious program consists not only of worship services, but seminars and workshops, prayer meetings, retreats, and special religious holiday observances. Generally, a facility will employ one full-time chaplain and maintain contracts with other clergy members or religious organizations. This combination provides a full range of religious programs that enables inmates to practice their religious beliefs to the greatest extent possible during confinement. In addition, volunteers from the community customarily devote considerable time to supplementing the programs provided by the institution.

RELIGIOUS PROGRAM

Chapel. A small chapel should be provided that seats a minimum of 15 people and is used exclusively for religious services. It need not be ornate and should contain no fixed denominational artifacts. About 350 square feet is usually sufficient for both seating and ceremonial activity. The chapel should be located so that inmates do not have to pass through other program areas to gain access. If it is located adjacent to a multi-purpose auditorium with a movable partition separating the two areas, the number of people who can attend religious services increases manyfold. This arrangement is also cost-efficient.

A small storage room adjacent to the chapel should be provided for liturgical supplies and artifacts.

Offices. Three offices, each occupying 120 square feet, are recommended for use by chaplains and clerks and for recordkeeping.

Lobby/Waiting Area. A lobby of about 150 square feet should be provided that leads to the offices and the chapel. This area also serves as a waiting room for inmates who wish to see the chaplain. An alternative is to provide a larger room of approximately 250 square feet to serve the auditorium as well as the chapel.

Toilet. A three-fixture facility should be located off of the lobby. A larger facility should be provided if the lobby also serves the auditorium.

The right of religious expression is a constitutional guarantee, and the courts have upheld vigorously the right of inmates to be given reasonable opportunities to pursue their religious beliefs during confinement. Thus, correctional facilities must offer flexible religious programs that will allow all inmates to exercise their religious beliefs.

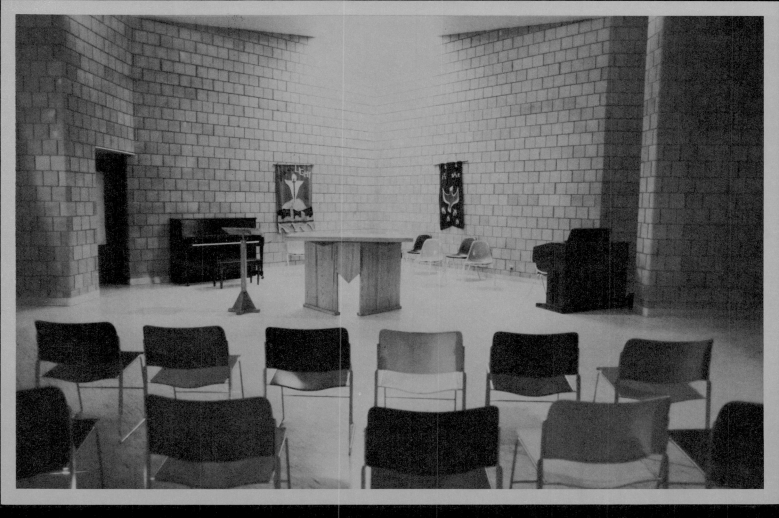

The chapel need not be ornate and should contain no fixed artifacts so that it can be

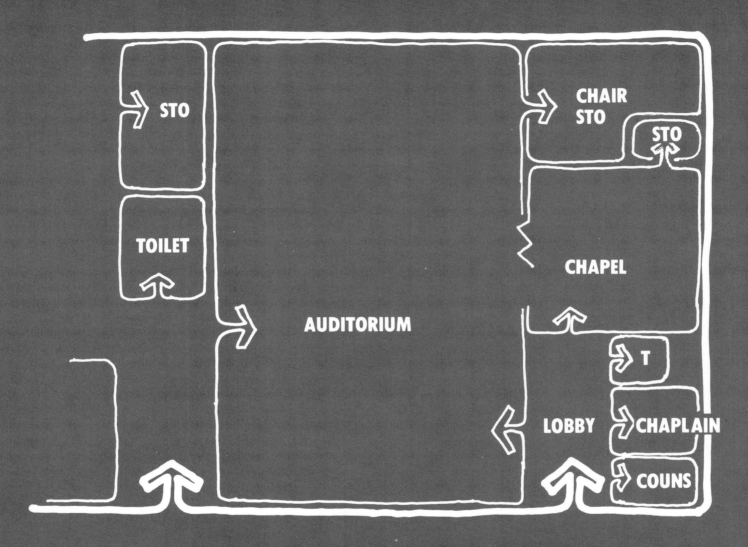

CHAPEL/AUDITORIUM

Multi-use areas are not dedicated for any single activity but instead serve various functions for both inmates and staff. A wide variety of programs and activities occur throughout the institution each day, including meetings, entertainment, special programs, and recreational activities. Some of these are conducted by volunteer organizations such as the Osborne Association, the Salvation Army, and the Volunteers of America. The facility thus should have several multi-purpose areas or spaces of different sizes to accommodate the groups participating in such activities.

Some planners create distinct space for volunteer activities near the facility's front entrance to keep volunteers away from the Institution's inner security zones. Experience has shown, however, that such space tends to be underutilized and thus very costly.

Auditorium. The auditorium is used for movies, ceremonies, plays, concerts, and other types of entertainment for large groups of inmates or staff.

The auditorium is the major multi-use space for large groups within the facility and should be

MULTI-USE AREAS

located near the major inmate circulation paths and adjacent to other multi-use rooms. A flat floor and movable seating are recommended so that the space can be used for a variety of activities. A raised stage, while not essential, is also useful. A movable partition separating the auditorium from the chapel allows additional seating for chapel activities. If located adjacent to other

functions in a similar manner, the auditorium can also be used for expanding those activities.

For a 500-capacity institution, the auditorium should be about 2,000 square feet and hold a minimum of 300 people, or 60 percent of the inmate population. This size should be adequate for most large institutional functions. On those rare occasions when a larger group is assembled, the gymnasium can be used.

Storage Room. An area of approximately 300 square feet should be provided for storing chairs and stage equipment. It is best located adjacent to the stage area, where it can also serve as a dressing room for performances.

Other Multi-Use Spaces. In addition to the auditorium, gymnasium, and visiting room, all of which can serve as multi-use space, there should be several other rooms of different sizes. A good combination would be one 200-square-foot room, two 300-square-foot rooms, and one 450-square-foot room. The ideal location for these rooms is adjacent to the auditorium where they can function as "breakout" rooms to which segments of larger groups can go for seminars and discussions.

In addition to the auditorium, gymnasium, and visiting room, all of which can serve as multi-use space, there should be several other rooms of different sizes. A good combination would be one 200-square-foot room, two 300-square-foot rooms, and one 450-square-foot room.

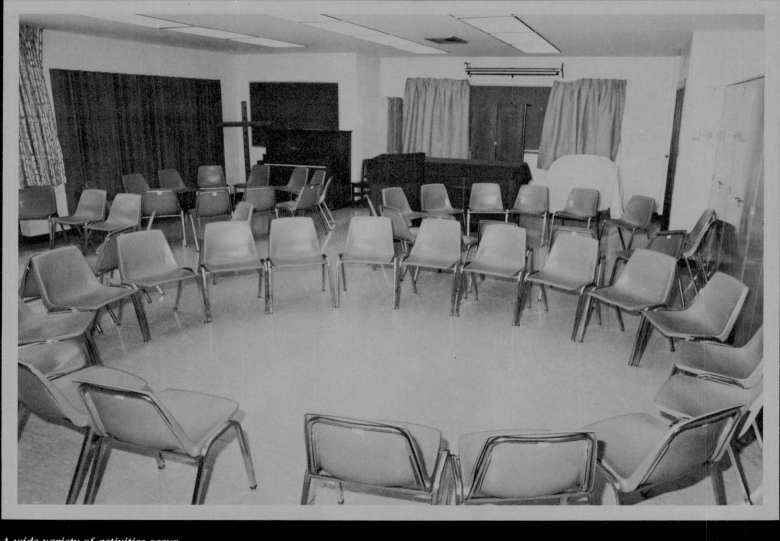

*A wide variety of activities occur
throughout the institution each day
including meetings, entertainment, and
special programs. Some are conducted by
volunteers from the community. The facility
should have several multi-use areas to
accommodate such events.*

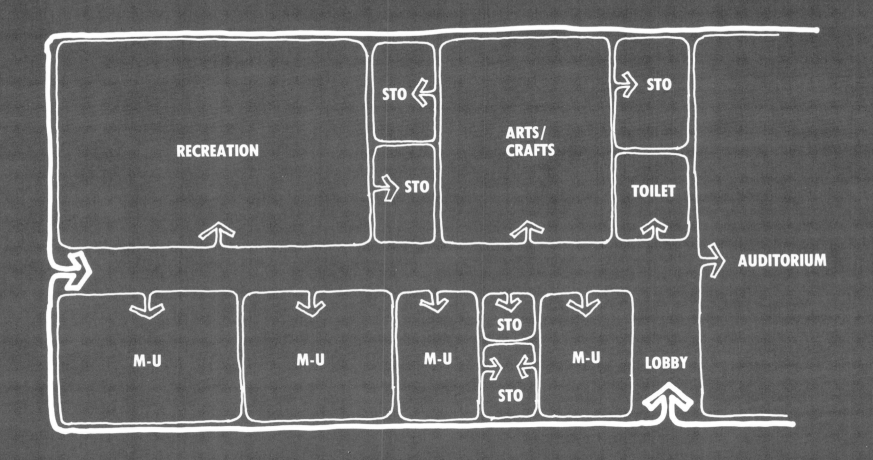

MULTI-USE/
INDOOR RECREATION

The mission of an industrial program in a correctional facility is to employ inmates in constructive activities, foster good work habits, and provide training opportunities in a variety of marketable skills. By providing employment opportunities, an industrial work program also reduces the idleness otherwise inherent in correctional facilities. An institufor 500 inmates can often employ as much as 45 to 50 percent of its inmate population in an industrial production program.

The choice of industrial programs will depend on a number of factors. Many states, as well as the federal government, have passed laws restricting the markets to which correctional industry programs can sell their products; these laws must be carefully researched. Consideration must also be given to the marketability of skills learned in different programs and the existing skill levels of the inmate population.

Staffing requirements include training and supervisory personnel as well as support services personnel such as accountants, purchasing agents, warehousemen, and quality assurance specialists. The number of

INDUSTRIAL PROGRAM

staff supervising inmates varies by the type of industry. A metal factory, for example, typically will employ one foreman for every 10 to 20 inmates, while a computer programming industry requires one supervisor for every 4 to 5 inmates.

The industrial program is located within the institution's perimeter security and should have a loading dock to facilitate deliveries and shipments of products. Although this program need not be located directly on major inmate circulation paths, good access by inmates is essential. It is also desirable to locate the in-

dustries area adjacent to the vocational training area. Industrial activities and vocational training programs change over the years and adjacent locations provide greater flexibility to convert one to the other as the need arises.

The industrial area includes factory space, warehouse space, and space for offices and toilets. The total area needed will depend on the number and type of industrial operations planned and the projected inmate employment levels. Planners often determine what types of industrial programs will be implemented and the number of inmates those industries will employ before planning the space. If correctional administrators have not decided what industries to operate, it is suggested that a large open shell be constructed with no floor and a minimum ceiling height of 12 feet. The appropriate partitions, utilities, and floor slab or slabs can be constructed once the program decisions have been made. Indeed, this latter method is often the best approach, considering the long lead time from initial planning to program operation and the rapidly changing market conditions that will often affect product lines.

Although the space required for industrial programs will vary, a rule of thumb is to allow 300 square feet of space for each inmate who will be working in industries at any one time. This allowance is usually sufficient for factory, warehouse, office, and toilet spaces. The industry building should be placed on the site to enable future expansion. This reduces the risk associated with using a rule-of-thumb area allowance. Offices and toilet facilities should be near the entrance to the industrial workplace to monitor inmate traffic easily.

A well-managed industrial program employs inmates in constructive activities, fosters good work habits, provides valuable training opportunities, and reduces idleness.

Although the space required for industrial programs will vary, a rule of thumb is to allow 300 square feet of space for each inmate who will be working in industries at any one time. This allowance is usually sufficient for factory, warehouse, office, and toilet space.

5
ADMINISTRATIVE
FUNCTIONS

The purpose of the administrative program is to provide leadership and support for an orderly and effectively operated correctional institution. Facilities needed for this program include offices for business, personnel, training, and information management, as well as executive staff functions.

The administrative offices should be located close to the institution's front entrance where they will be readily accessible to the public. Many people using this entrance will be conducting business only in the administration area and will not need to go any farther into the facility. The administration building, however, should be inside the institution's security perimeter. This minimizes both the physical and psychological distance between upper management and the programs and operations. If the chief executive officer and other administrative staff are located outside the secure perimeter, a practice which has been traditional, they are less likely to have direct contact with line staff and inmates. As a general rule, the less contact, the less effective the manage-

ADMINISTRATIVE OFFICES

ment. Wardens and other top-level administrators who "walk and talk" frequently with staff and inmates are usually more effective managers who promote high levels of inmate and staff morale.

Executive Offices

The chief executive officer (CEO), also known as the warden or superintendent, exercises ultimate authority over the institution. This officer and his or her direct support staff are the most frequently visited personnel in the institution, and access to their offices must be readily available from both inside and outside the institution.

Institutional responsibilities are usually divided among the assistant wardens. The function of public information officer should be assigned to one person who is a principal member of the warden's staff, such as an executive or administrative assistant. A position for legal counsel may also be needed, although some facilities assign this function to a paralegal.

It is often desirable to locate executive offices so that they provice good visibility of the institution compound.

Waiting Room. A single waiting room of about 150 square feet should be centrally located to serve both the executive and business offices. Typically, a secretary/receptionist will be stationed in this area to provide secretarial support to the administrative staff.

Executive Offices.   The chief ex-

The administration building should be inside the institution's security perimeter. This minimizes both the physical and psychological distance between upper management and the programs and operations.

The chief executive officer's private office should be large enough to accommodate a meeting with eight people. A larger conference room for up to 20 people should be located in the executive suite.

ecutive officer should have a private office of approximately 250 square feet, large enough to hold meetings or interviews and accommodate up to eight people. An adjoining 150-square-foot space should be provided for the chief executive's secretary. Individual offices, ranging from 100 to 150 square feet each, should be located nearby for other members of the executive management team, such as the executive assistant, public information officer, and assistant wardens. (Depending on local policy, offices for assistant wardens are sometimes located more centrally to inmate activity and program areas to facilitate closer supervision.) In addition, a minimum space of 300 square feet should be provided for secretarial services.

Conference Room. A conference room that will comfortably accommodate up to 20 people should be provided for meetings and seminars. Larger groups can use the staff training or multi-use rooms.

Toilets. Appropriate toilet facilities should be provided in the administration building to serve the executive offices and other administrative staff.

Some facilities have been designed to provide the CEO with an unobstructed view of the inner compound.

Business Office

The business office is responsible for all financial transactions of the institution and is staffed by specialists in accounting, budgeting, procurement, property management, and contracting procedures. Since the staff must frequently conduct business with the public, their offices should be located adjacent to the waiting room.

Business Manager's Office. The business manager should have a private office with about 120 square feet located near the entrance to the business office.

Cashier's Office. The cashier should also have a private office with about 120 square feet, constructed in a secure fashion and designed with a small pass-through window to a major staff circulation corridor. The office should be equipped with a safe for holding money and checks.

Open Office Space. Other business staff, including clerical support personnel, should be located in an open office of about 1,500 square feet. Dividers with sound-absorbing surfaces should be used to subdivide the space. This area contains files, catalogs, and office equipment used in day-to-day activities, including

computer terminals.

Work/Storage Room. A dual-purpose work/storage room with about 250 square feet should be available for such items as supplies, files, and copying machines. Other noisy equipment should also be located in this room to prevent noise from disturbing staff and visitors.

Administrative Security Offices

The chief of security and the supervisory security staff oversee one of the most important functions in a correctional institution and require adequate space to carry out their various responsibilities, which include the supervision of correctional officers, conducting interviews concerning incidents and rules violations, writing reports, and meeting with members of the local law enforcement community.

While offices for security personnel can be located in a number of different places, they should be reasonably accessible to certain heavily used staff service facilities. These are typically clustered in one area and include the staff lounge and assembly room, staff library, personnel offices,

Most business office functions can take place in a large open space. Dividers with sound absorbing surfaces can be used to subdivide the area.

and staff training room. These offices should be located on the main circulation floor level, typically the first floor, and situated so that staff have a clear view into the main compound.

An office with 120 square feet should be provided for the chief of security, and an office with 300 square feet, adjacent to the chief's office, should be provided for supervisory security staff and clerical personnel.

Personnel Office

The personnel department is responsible for administering numerous programs related to personnel policy, recruitment, staff training, position management, recordkeeping, and various other activities. The offices for this department should be convenient to members of the public looking into employment, and also situated to encourage good interaction between staff in the department and line staff.

In many institutions, the personnel officer directly coordinates staff training, but this practice is declining because of the increased emphasis on upgrading the professional skills of correctional workers and the consequent need to employ a training of-

ficer on a full-time basis.

The staff complement for this program usually includes a personnel officer, a personnel specialist and a clerk. In some facilities, the personnel officer reports directly to the warden. In other cases however, an assistant warden supervises the personnel activities.

The personnel offices should be near the staff lounge, locker room, and training facilities. Two private offices, each with about 120 square feet, should be provided for conducting small meetings or private interviews. An open work area with 250 square feet should be located adjacent to these offices for secretarial staff. This area can also serve as a waiting room and a place for staff and applicants to pick up forms and pamphlets. A bulletin board should be prominently displayed to post announcements. An adjoining 75-square-foot room should be provided for secure storage.

Security personnel use their offices for such activities as conducting interviews, reviewing incident reports and meeting with members of law enforcement agencies.

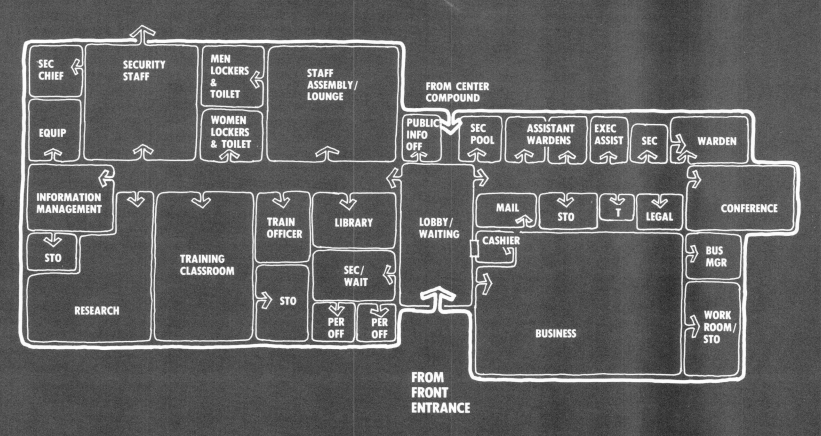

SEC CHIEF

SECURITY STAFF

MEN LOCKERS & TOILET

STAFF ASSEMBLY/ LOUNGE

FROM CENTER COMPOUND

EQUIP

WOMEN LOCKERS & TOILET

PUBLIC INFO OFF

SEC POOL

ASSISTANT WARDENS

EXEC ASSIST

SEC

WARDEN

INFORMATION MANAGEMENT

TRAIN OFFICER

LIBRARY

LOBBY/ WAITING

MAIL

STO

T

LEGAL

CONFERENCE

STO

CASHIER

BUS MGR

TRAINING CLASSROOM

SEC/ WAIT

RESEARCH

STO

PER OFF

PER OFF

BUSINESS

WORK ROOM/ STO

FROM FRONT ENTRANCE

ADMINISTRATION

Training Department

There is a growing and widespread recognition that effective training programs are essential if correctional staff are to respond to the challenges that lie ahead. While new and better institutions are sorely needed, along with many other resources, a higher level of staff professionalism is undoubtedly the single most important factor necessary for improving and advancing correctional programs. Administration officials should exert maximum effort to obtain the support and resources needed for the operation of a professional training program. Virtually all correctional managers agree that a qualified, well-trained professional staff is more effective than a significantly larger complement of less qualified, less skilled staff members. It is often hard to convince key decisionmakers of this truth, but the effort must continue. From a purely pragmatic point of view, better trained and more highly skilled staff are substantially less likely to render the state (and the taxpayer) vulnerable to costly adverse court judgments. The long-term benefits to

STAFF TRAINING AND SERVICES

the public, while more difficult to envision, are no less significant.

To operate an adequate training program, a classroom that will comfortably accommodate up to 40 people should be provided in a space of at least 500 square feet. Provisions should be made so that the room can be darkened to present slides, films, or closed-circuit television training programs. While most training can be conducted in this classroom, addi-

tional training needs can usually be met by using the various multi-use spaces available throughout modern institutions. The training classroom should be available for other activities when not needed for its primary function.

In addition, there should be an office with approximately 120 square feet for the training officer, and a storage room with about 100 square feet for copying machines, audiovisual equipment, supplies, and files. These rooms should be adjacent to one another.

Special emphasis should be placed on training all new employees, especially correctional officers and others who will be working directly with inmates. Training courses will be diverse, ranging from courses in security procedures, firearms use, self-defense, supervision of inmates, and counseling techniques to report writing, staff supervision, and financial operations. The department may be staffed with a training officer, with clerical support provided by secretarial personnel in the executive office area. Other staff members with specific expertise are often used to help develop and conduct special

Virtually all correctional managers agree that a qualified, well-trained, professional staff is more effective than a significantly larger complement of less qualified, less skilled staff members. It is often hard to convince key decision-makers of this truth, but the effort must continue.

training programs. In addition, the facility will probably contract with outside specialists to provide training that cannot be accomplished in-house.

While some institutions may have sufficient justification for constructing a special area for firearms instruction, most agencies can, at a considerable savings, take advantage of existing firearms training facilities operated by local law enforcement agencies. The correctional facility's gym can be used for training staff in self-defense techniques. Thus, staff training needs should require only the special construction of a classroom, office, and storage space. These facilities should be located near the personnel department and the staff lounge.

Staff Services

A correctional institution should have a staff library to make available information and reference materials that support the personnel and training programs. To be accessible to staff, the library is usually located near the staff training area and the staff lounge. It should be well stocked with carefully selected, up-

to-date books, periodicals, and other reference materials. A space of 250 square feet is usually adequate for accommodating a reading area and displaying and stocking appropriate materials. While full-time supervision is not needed, a staff member should be assigned responsibility for overseeing its operation.

A combination staff assembly room and lounge should be provided as a place for staff to relax, eat, converse, or read, and to assemble before starting to work. This room is one of the few places in the facility where staff congregate. It should be located near the personnel offices, mail room, lockers, and cashier's office, areas where most staff go regularly. The room should be approximately 800 square feet, and have a bulletin board to prominently display information and news of interest to staff. Vending machines, a sink, a small refrigerator, a microwave oven, and counter space should be provided, as well as tables

and chairs. Frequently, arrangements are made for in-house mail delivery to this area. This area can also serve as the staging point for assembling the institution riot or tactical squad.

Separate locker rooms for male and female staff should be provided adjacent to the staff lounge for staff members to change into their uniforms and store their street clothing. These facilities usually range between 200 and 350 square feet each, depending on the number of male and female staff employed. Each locker room should be equipped with toilet and shower facilities.

There is an increasing tendency among some administrations to provide space for credit unions, employee unions, and other related activities in addition to the staff services described above. Planners should carefully assess this trend and determine during the early development stages whether such facilities will be included in the new institution.

The staff library should be well stocked with carefully selected, up-to-date books, periodicals, and other reference materials important for staff of a correctional facility.

On-going staff training is an essential
element of a well-run correctional facility
(opposite). Virtually all correctional
managers agree that a qualified, well-
trained professional staff is more effective
than a significantly larger complement of
less qualified, less skilled staff members. The
staff assembly room (above) should provide
a place for staff to relax, eat, read,
converse, and gather before starting to
work.

Information Management Office

The information management office maintains and updates a variety of information, including information concerning the admission, transfer, and discharge of inmates. The staff of this office are also responsible for sentence computation and processing of detainers. To carry out these duties, they must maintain such records as court commitment documents and judicial orders relating to dates of confinement and anticipated release. Much of their work results from legal obligations.

In addition, collecting and managing other kinds of information has become increasingly important. Much of this data is inmate-related and includes demographics, work history, social and educational background, prior record, and medical and mental health status, as well as information on the inmate's confinement, such as programming, furloughs, and disciplinary reports. Greater use is being made of automatic information systems to store and retrieve information that enhances management decision-

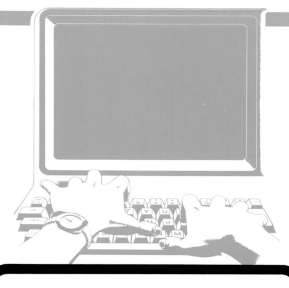

INFORMATION MANAGEMENT AND RESEARCH

making and programming for the inmate population. These systems may also be used to monitor information such as training provided to staff. Not only is the data helpful to correctional administrators, it also provides a solid data base from which correctional research can be conducted.

Some jurisdictions include within the duties of this office the management of additional information systems, such as fiscal data, property management, and personnel activities.

A full-time information management officer and one or two assistants should have responsibility for managing this office. The exact number of additional technical staff will vary, depending on the amount of information desired and the complexity of the system. Since the confidentiality of this information must be assured, inmates must never work in this office.

Some correctional systems locate their information systems in a headquarters or regional office, rather than at each institution, and furnish small data stations at various locations in the institutions. If data collection and management activities are carried out at the institution, however, the following spaces should be provided:

- Information Management Office. One 500-square-foot office should be located in the administrative area adjacent to the research area so that data is easily accessible to researchers. The office must be

The envelope of these three information management rooms—office, storage, and equipment—should be secure to protect the confidentiality of records and minimize the potential for sabotage or theft. Access codes and locks for all terminals provide an additional layer of security.

large enough to accommodate all staff associated with these activities.

- Storage Room. A separate room with 200 square feet should be designed for storing inactive files, unless all records are stored in a computer system.
- Equipment Room. An equipment room, between 300 and 500 square feet in size, should be located adjacent to the information management office. It should be designed to dampen the sound from noisy equipment such as computers and duplication and teletype machines. The exact size will depend on the number of users at any one time and the type and amount of equipment housed there.

The envelope of these three rooms—office, storage, and equipment—should be secure to protect the confidentiality of records and minimize the potential for sabotage or theft. Access codes and locks for all terminals provide an additional layer of security. Computer-type flooring should also be considered for these rooms.

Research Office

The need for greater knowledge about the criminal justice system as a whole is well known. The need within the correctional system component is no less great, and correctional managers should be encouraged to invest at least a small part of their resources in the scientific collection of information and its analysis.

While even a small expense for research activities may seem exorbitant in the short run, in the long run these costs are often more than recovered. Better information leads to better decisions, and correctional managers face a constant stream of decision-making concerning programs and procedures. Deciding whether a program should be continued, expanded, cut back, eliminated, or otherwise modified is a regular part of correctional administrative life. Such determinations will yield more cost-effective use of available resources if made in the light of solid, well-analyzed information. Good research on program effectiveness, when shared, can also be helpful to the broader field of corrections.

Some correctional institutions conduct their own research and have one or more full-time staff devoted to this work. Others contract for or augment their research with outside resources such as local universities, foundations, or special research institutes. Research staff are frequently assisted by interns from nearby colleges and universities.

If permanent full-time research staff will not be assigned to the facility, researchers can usually use various multi-purpose space at the institution. If there are full-time research positions, a work room should be located adjacent to the information management office, facilitating the research staff's access to data. An open office area of 300 to 500 square feet should adequately accommodate the research staff and student interns, as well as any computer terminals that may be used.

The information management office maintains and updates a variety of information files. The use of computer technology aids these functions greatly.

6
SERVICE FACILITIES

The service facilities in a correctional institution generally consist of the maintenance, safety, and sanitation departments, warehouses, a fire station, a garage and, if provided, the power house. These facilities provide support services to ensure that the institution is clean, safe, and humane and that mechanical and utility systems operate without interruption. A correctional facility contains many buildings and pieces of mechanical equipment that cannot operate properly without frequent attention from skilled specialists. Maintenance shops must be provided and they should be grouped in one area. Usually, shops are provided for carpentry/cabinetwork, electrical/electronic maintenance, heating/air conditioning maintenance, plumbing, metal working, painting, and landscaping. In addition to ensuring proper maintenance and operation of the physical plant, the shops furnish inmates with opportunities for on-the-job training in marketable skills.

Open maintenance shops may be designed for multiple use, provided the requirements for each function are adequately met. The better prac-

PLANT MAINTENANCE DEPARTMENT

tice, however, is to design specific space for each shop. Staff and inmates assigned to the shops should have access to the vocational training facilities that may offer programs related to maintenance.

A basic maintenance staff for an institution with 500 inmates includes a plant maintenance supervisor, a clerk, and one or more specialists in each maintenance area. Since inattention to proper building maintenance has costly implications for the future, it is essential to staff this facility properly. In most instances, each shop

employs several inmates who do much of the maintenance work under close staff supervision. Some items, however, such as locks, equipment for the armory and control center, and other security-related or potentially hazardous items, should never be maintained by inmates.

The maintenance department is usually adjacent to the truck loading dock and vehicular sally port. The optimal location is one that provides outside access to the grounds and all buildings, as well as easy access to the food service, laundry, and industries areas, which generally require high levels of maintenance.

Shops. The shops require 5,000 to 6,000 square feet of space for general maintenance and training inmates. The clear ceiling height should be 12 feet to accommodate the handling of large equipment and supplies. Overhead doors should be provided to enable installation of large equipment items and movement of materials. Certain tools such as saws and planes should be equipped with sawdust collectors to minimize dust in the atmosphere.

Proper tool storage is extremely

Open maintenance shops may be designed for multiple use, provided the requirements for each function are adequately met. The better practice, however, is to design specific space for each shop. Staff and inmates assigned to the shops should have access to the vocational training facilities that may offer programs related to maintenance.

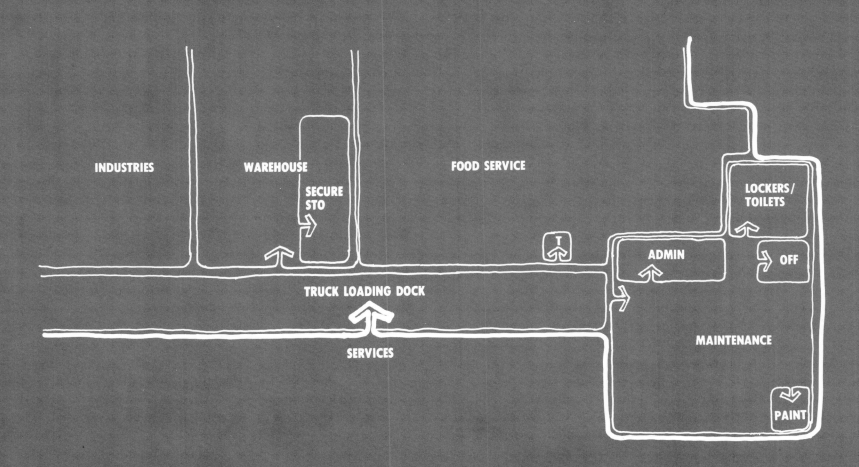

INDUSTRIES

WAREHOUSE

FOOD SERVICE

SECURE STO

LOCKERS/ TOILETS

ADMIN

OFF

TRUCK LOADING DOCK

MAINTENANCE

SERVICES

PAINT

SERVICE FACILITIES

Maintenance shops can be grouped in one area. Usually shops are provided for carpentry/cabinet work, electrical/electronic maintenance, plumbing, metal working, painting, and landscaping.

important; many tools can be used as lethal weapons or to facilitate escape attempts. A separately partitioned and secure room with about 150 square feet is needed for tool storage and should be provided with an issue window that can be securely closed and locked. Accountability of tools, especially small tools, is enhanced by the use of a "shadow board" that

reveals at a glance which tools, if any, are missing.

Most shops are located in large, open bay structures that have few separating partitions. Electronic shops, however, must be housed in a separate dust-free room. In addition, it is good practice to isolate carpentry shops because of the dust they generate. The use of separately partitioned

rooms also makes it easier to reduce unauthorized traffic in the shops, a provision very important to security.

Paint Storage. A separate paint storage room of approximately 20 square feet is required for the safe storage of paint materials. It must be located on an exterior wall and constructed with either an exterior door or an explosion release panel. Planners and designers should refer to the NFPA Life Safety Code for additional requirements, such as explosion-proof fixtures.

Administrator's Office. Approximately 120 square feet should be provided for the administrator's office and files. The office should be located at the entrance to the shops and afford a good view of these areas.

Support Staff Area. A room with 400 square feet should be located adjacent to the administrator's office to provide working space for up to six administrative support staff, including clerks and one or two draftsmen. Clerical and drafting work is usually done by inmates.

Toilets / Lockers. Appropriate toilet facilities with about a dozen lockers should be available for maintenance staff.

Proper tool storage is extremely important. A separately partitioned and secure room with an issue window is needed. Shadow boards that reveal at a glance any missing tools aid accountability.

A sound safety and sanitation program is a basic element in every correctional operation. The supervisor of the safety program is generally responsible for coordinating the institution's life safety program, including fire prevention and evacuation planning, emergency procedures, and control of the use of toxic substances. The sanitation program supervisor is customarily responsible for monitoring a variety of activities, with particular attention to food quality, pest control, and the water supply, and for ensuring that healthful sanitation practices are observed throughout the institution. Good sanitation, along with an orderly appearance, sets an important tone in the institution, helps promote a positive atmosphere, and conveys the administration's expectations about the quality of the operation. Conversely, poor sanitation often leads to a perception that the administration is careless and slipshod, which can foster serious problems and exacerbate others.

While many correctional agencies direct the safety and sanitation program from their central office, these programs are of such importance that

SAFETY AND SANITATION OFFICE

it is recommended they be supervised at each individual facility. Since these activities are so closely related, they can generally be managed by one individual with the assistance of one clerk, if possible, and common space can be provided for both functions.

The safety and sanitation office serves the entire institution and can be located in a variety of places. It is helpful to locate it not too distant from the truck loading dock to facilitate the movement of equipment and the delivery of supplies. It should also be reasonably accessible to the food service, canteen, laundry, industries, maintenance shops, vocational training shops, and warehouse areas, as these departments generally require more attention. Since chemicals and equipment are frequently stored in this department, it is usually located in the rear of the institution, often near the maintenance shops.

The sanitation and safety office requires approximately 350 square feet to accommodate its staff and files. An adjacent 200-square-foot space can be provided to store equipment and supplies and should be equipped with a sink, counter, and space for preparing certain chemicals.

Fire Protection

Fire safety is of paramount importance in the institution's safety program. Designers must plan the facility according to relevant codes, and administrators must ensure that the proper equipment is available and operational. Administrators must also establish a sound comprehensive fire

Good sanitation, along with orderly appearance, sets an important tone in the institution, helps promote a positive atmosphere, and conveys the administration's expectations about the quality of the operation. Conversely, poor sanitation often leads to a perception that the administration is careless and slipshod, which can foster serious problems and exacerbate others.

emergency policy, which should include thorough training and periodic fire drills for both staff and inmates. Frequently, an inmate fire crew is established and given special training.

The threat of fire in a correctional facility is particularly acute since the movement of inmates is restricted. Recognizing this problem, the National Fire Protection Association has promulgated a set of regulations specifically for new and existing deten-

tion and correctional occupancies. These were published for the first time in the 1981 edition of the NFPA *Life Safety Code,* Chapters 14 and 15. In addition, the National Bureau of Standards is developing a fire safety evaluation system to measure compliance with the code; this is to be included in the next edition of the *Life Safety Code.*

Depending on the institution's proximity to a local fire department

and the department's capability and willingness to provide fire protection to the institution, it may or may not be necessary to provide a fire station and fire truck at the facility. Even if the institution provides its own fire protection department, however, coordination with the local fire department is essential to augment service.

If a fire station is included in the facility's design, it should be located outside the secure perimeter since vehicles inside the perimeter pose an escape hazard. The station should also be close to the vehicular sally port so that fire equipment and personnel can enter quickly. It is often located in one of the vehicle bays in an outside garage. For a facility of this size, a 24-foot pump truck is usually adequate for fighting most fires. A bay with about 800 square feet and a minimum depth of 40 feet is needed to house the fire truck and provide space for maintenance, hose-drying racks, and ancillary fire fighting equipment. The bay should be constructed with an overhead door 12 feet high and 14 feet in width to allow adequate clearance for the truck.

The safety and sanitation office serves the entire institution. It should be located near the truck loading dock, and be reasonably accessible to food service, canteen, laundry, industries, maintenance shops, vocational training shops, and warehouse areas as these departments generally require more attention.

Garage

The garage, normally located outside the perimeter, provides space for vehicle maintenance and storage for landscaping machinery and supplies. It is usually under the supervision of the chief garage vehicle mechanic. Facilities include the following:

- Three 800-square-foot bays for vehicle maintenance. One bay should have an overhead door and vehicular lifts for servicing.
- A larger bay of about 1,000 square feet, equipped with an overhead door, for landscaping vehicles and storing landscaping supplies such as seed and garden hoses.
- An 800-square-foot bay for the fire truck, if one is required.
- One 250-square-foot office located between the vehicular and landscaping bays, constructed with view windows to facilitate supervision of activities in the garage.
- An equipment and supply storage room of approximately 200 square feet, located adjacent to the office.
- Toilet facilities, located near the office to serve both staff and inmates who work in the area.

GARAGE AND WAREHOUSES

Warehouses

Space must be provided for the general storage of supplies needed for the ongoing operation of the institution. The amount of space is influenced by such factors as the inventory, turnover rate, delivery schedules, and existing storage systems. The warehouse staff typically consists of a warehouse supervisor and one or two staff assistants, who are often augmented by a cadre of carefully selected inmates.

Except for low-level medium security institutions, two general supply warehouses should be provided, one outside the institution's security perimeter and one inside the perimeter. These warehouses are distinct from the individual kitchen, industries, medical, and canteen storage areas. Supplies for those four operations are transported directly to their respective warehouses on delivery. Generally, all other supplies are delivered to the outside warehouse where they can be inspected and stored for a short period of time before being transferred inside the secure perimeter by institution-owned trucks. This procedure reduces the possibility of introducing contraband into the institution. Items that will be used outside of the secure perimeter remain stored in the outside warehouse.

Outside Warehouse

The outside warehouse should be located adjacent to the secure perimeter near the vehicular sally

Except for low-level medium security institutions, two general supply warehouses should be provided, one outside the institution's security perimeter and one inside the perimeter. These warehouses are distinct from the individual kitchen, industries, medical, and canteen storage areas. . . . Generally, all other supplies are delivered to the outside warehouse where they can be inspected and stored for a short period of time before being transferred inside the secure perimeter by institution-owned trucks.

The garage is located outside the perimeter fence. It provides bays for vehicle maintenance, space for a fire truck (if provided), and storage for landscaping machinery and supplies.

port. It is often located in the same area as the garage/fire station, power house (if any), and other "outside" structures. It should not be located near the front entrance or staff and visitor's parking lot because it would detract from the appearance of these areas and interfere with circulation patterns.

For an institution with a capacity for 500 inmates, a warehouse with approximately 1,500 square feet of open space and a minimum ceiling height of 12 feet is needed. The warehouse should be equipped with steel storage shelving and a truck loading dock with both overhead doors and a pedestrian door.

One 250-square-foot office should be situated so that the receiving officer can observe both the loading dock and the warehouse area.

A toilet facility equipped with a toilet, wash basin, and service sink should be located adjacent to the office. If the warehouse is sited near other outside structures, the toilet facilities can be shared with other services.

Inside Warehouse

The inside warehouse is used for the long-term storage of all items not delivered directly to certain specialized departments. It should have about 4,500 square feet of area and a 12-foot-high clear ceiling. Provisions should include an adjacent truck dock with both an overhead and pedestrian door.

Since inmates help operate the inside warehouse, goods stored there are generally more accessible. Secure storage for tools and equipment that could be used for escape attempts is essential. A securely locked room with 400 square feet will usually satisfy this requirement; sometimes the separating partition is made of expanded metal mesh applied to steel studs.

The outside warehouse (opposite) is often located in the same area as the garage/fire station, power house (if any), and other outside structures. The inside warehouse (above) is used for long-term storage of all items not delivered directly to departments with their own storage area. It should have about 4500 square feet and a 12-foot high clear ceiling. Both garage and outside warehouse (below) should be convenient to the rear sally port.

For the most part, utility systems for correctional facilities are like those provided for other types of domiciliary or residential housing facilities. The following is not a complete discussion of utility systems, but rather an effort to highlight important features of these systems specifically related to correctional institutions.

Electrical System

Since the electrical system provides an essential service to the facility, any disruption of this system can cause serious security problems. Consequently, it is crucial that staff skilled in the maintenance and repair of this system be available to ensure minimal disruptions and to perform immediate repairs.

Electrical power is normally distributed from a central transformer and switching station that frequently is located outside the security perimeter, particularly if there is a power house. Sometimes the switching station is located in a building inside the perimeter, usually near the truck dock, in which case the station should be protected with a security door and lock.

UTILITY SYSTEMS AND POWER HOUSE

Traditionally, staff have controlled all lighting throughout the institution. Increasingly, however, light switches easily accessible to inmates are being installed in most areas within the facility. Some systems provide individual switches in inmate rooms and in the multi-purpose spaces in the housing units. If administrators are concerned about inmates having access to light switches in housing units, central switches that only staff operate can be provided.

An emergency electrical generating system is essential to ensure a continuous power supply for vital services, especially the control center and other operations essential to maintaining the facility's security. The generator should be installed with an automatic switch-over capability unless the facility has a central power plant staffed with full-time operators who can quickly switch to emergency generation. During the switch-over period, the battery-operated telephone system and walkie-talkies will be used to maintain the security of the facility. Usually, a single 500-kilowatt generator is adequate for a 500-bed correctional institution. This generator is not sized to carry the entire electrical load, but rather provides for emergency, security-related service and partial service for certain other electrical demands. Facilities with electric heat and other unusual demands should consider installing additional emergency generating capacity. For larger systems it is also a good practice to have more than one generator so that if one is disabled, the second can handle the most pressing electrical needs.

While the electrical system must

An emergency electrical generating system is essential to ensure a continuous power supply for vital services, especially the Control Center and other operations essential to maintaining the facility's security. The generator should be installed with an automatic switch-over capability unless the facility has a central power plant staffed with full-time operators who can quickly switch to emergency generation.

water tank is needed. Otherwise, an elevated or pressurized water tank is required on-site. At a minimum, the tank should store a five-day emergency backup water supply, or 575 thousand to 750 thousand gallons. In addition, provisions must be made to insure sufficient water for fire protection in accordance with the code of the National Fire Protection Association (NFPA).

As in many other types of facilities, water supply valves are located throughout the institution. In correctional facilities it is particularly important to design the water supply and distribution system to separate small groups of housing from the water supply lines. This design permits troubled areas to be isolated without shutting off entire buildings. It is recommended that in housing units a bank or wing of up to 12 to 15 rooms have a separate water cut-off valve to minimize disruption in water service.

Sewage System

It usually is preferable to connect the facility to a local sewage system, thus conserving the staff time needed to operate and maintain a separate treatment plant. If this is not feasible, an on-site sewage treatment system must be installed and staffed by qualified personnel who will ensure that the service meets all applicable environmental pollution control standards. Generally, between 80 and 90 percent of the total water consumption will need to be treated, so long as the balance of the water is returned to the soil, largely through landscape irrigation, a separate storm sewer exists, and no farming takes place on the institutional grounds.

A bar screen should be installed between the sewer line and the local utility line or at the point where the sewer line enters on-site treatment facilities. This prevents blockage if inappropriate materials are flushed into the system by the inmates. Wherever pipes exceeding 10 inches in diameter, such as storm sewer pipes, cross under the security perimeter, a manifold system of pipes no greater than 10 inches in diameter should be used to prevent the possibility of inmate escapes.

Heating, Ventilating, and Air Conditioning

Heating, ventilating, and air conditioning (HVAC) systems, while generally the same as those for non-correctional facilities, require security features to prevent inmates from tampering with the units. Also, security steel bar grilles must be placed inside air ducts wherever the ducts penetrate a security barrier.

In warm climates, air conditioning should be carefully considered in certain areas of an institution, including the housing units, the dining room, the hospital, and the administration building. While there are certain operational and maintenance costs associated with an air conditioning system, there are also advantages not directly measurable, that may significantly outweigh the financial expense. Air conditioning can help minimize the normal tensions of confinement that inevitably escalate in a hot, humid environment, thus preventing the violence and disturbances that too often occur during hot weather and exact high costs not only in repairs but in injuries and, sometimes, loss of life for both staff and inmates.

Planners may want to consider installing smoke exhaust systems and/or automatic damper systems to reduce the spread of smoke as in-

In warm climates, air conditioning should be carefully considered in certain areas of the institution, including the housing units, the dining room, the hospital, and the administration building. While there are certain operational and maintenance costs associated with an air conditioning system, there are also advantages not directly measurable that may significantly outweigh the financial expense.

tegral parts of the HVAC system. The NFPA Life Safety Code and local codes should be consulted.

Solid Waste Disposal

Solid waste disposal requirements for correctional facilities are generally the same as those for other types of facilities. If sufficient land is available, an institution landfill program may be feasible even though regulations for such an operation are becoming increasingly stringent. In most facilities, solid waste is disposed of by a local contractor who removes the waste from the institution trash compactor. Proper security procedures must be enforced to prevent escapes. Typically, trash is removed from an institution immediately following a full count of all inmates.

Alternative Fuels and Energy Conservation

The sharply rising costs of energy over the last decade have had a dramatic impact on the operational budgets of all facilities and have made everyone sensitive to the need to undertake conservation measures and carefully assess the costs of alternative sources of energy.

Planners are strongly encouraged to conduct a cost/benefit analysis of alternative fuels, including related life-cycle costs, before deciding on the most appropriate fuel source for new facilities. In addition to analyzing the more conventional sources such as natural gas, coal, and electricity, it may be appropriate to consider such energy sources as geothermal, solid waste products, or solar. While the use of solar energy is compatible with the operation of a correctional facility, experience to date has shown that the costs associated with constructing and operating active solar systems have outweighed their benefits, although solar heating of domestic hot water has proved efficient. Thus far, passive solar systems appear to be the most practical and cost-efficient solar method for space heating.

Correctional administrators should stress the importance of using energy conservation measures and managing fuel consumption effectively to eliminate waste. This can be accomplished through the use of added insulation, automated temperature control systems, energy recovery systems for such operations as the laundry, and economizers on boiler exhausts. In addition, fuel management measures such as "peak shaving" of the electrical load can reduce energy costs by avoiding high peak-demand charges.

Power House

Traditional correctional facilities were usually equipped with a power house located outside the secure perimeter fence system. Many contemporary facilities use decentralized heating and air conditioning package units. While a central power house requires greater initial capital costs than package units, the operational and maintenance costs of a power house may be less. A life-cycle cost analysis of both options should be conducted to determine which is most appropriate. The analysis should include consideration that centralized power plants usually require around-the-clock operators. Either system is ordinarily satisfactory from a security standpoint, as long as prudent measures are undertaken such as locating package units on building roofs where they are not easily accessible to inmates.

Planners are strongly encouraged to conduct a cost-benefit analysis of alternative fuels, including related life-cycle costs, before deciding on the most appropriate fuel source for a new facility.

7
SECURITY FEATURES

The primary obligation of a correctional system is to ensure the custody and safekeeping of persons committed by the courts to a period of institutional confinement, while providing humane and safe environments for staff and inmates alike. At the same time, inmate programs and activities should be provided in an atmosphere that encourages inmates to use their period of confinement for personal growth and self-improvement.

The challenge for correctional managers is to plan a positive and balanced correctional program that reduces to the lowest possible levels the tensions and frustrations produced by both confinement and institutional living. To the degree this effort is successful, the need to rely on physical security features is lessened.

Correctional facility designers increasingly rely on a strong, extremely secure perimeter enclosure around the institution. The most common contemporary method is to use a double fence and integral electronic intrusion alarm devices, coupled with new types of concertina wire. Such fence systems are very satisfactory for the perimeter security, particularly

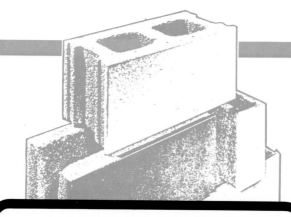

BUILDING SECURITY

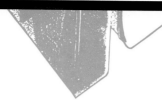

when mobile patrols are also used. The combination of these features usually eliminates the need for guard towers, which are costly to construct and exorbitantly costly to operate. In addition, since staff positions are usually in short supply, staff resources otherwise delegated to guard towers can be diverted to more productive assignments within the institution, further reducing the threat of escapes and testing of the perimeter security system.

A reliable perimeter security system allows inside operations to be more relaxed, with less need for constant observation of the inmate's every movement and a resulting reduction in both inmate and staff tensions. Such an atmosphere, coupled with sound programs, greatly enhances the prospects of positive experiences during confinement.

Another primary security "system" involves the perimeter enclosure or envelope—walls, ceilings and floors—of housing units. This feature is important for a number of reasons. During sleeping hours, fewer staff are usually available for supervision. Frequently, only one correctional officer may be on duty in each housing unit during this time, and if there is an inmate disturbance, it is important to contain the disturbance within the single building. In the event of general unrest, work stoppages, widespread violence, or potential broad-based disturbances, a secure building envelope gives staff the capability to lock inmates in their housing unit until the problem can be addressed and the emergency brought under control.

A secure housing perimeter, cou-

The perimeter enclosure or envelope of housing units—walls, ceilings, and floors—is a primary security system.

pled with a reliable and secure perimeter fence system, has other advantages. Traditional heavy-duty locking systems on individual room or cell doors become far less important. Many higher-level medium security institutions with strong housing and compound perimeters are operating successfully without these very expensive traditional locking systems.

In addition, costly architectural barriers that separate staff from inmates, such as individual control rooms in each housing module or secure partitions to create guards' corridors, can be eliminated. Barriers merely enable staff to observe the inmates under their control. This actually hinders effective supervision, which can come only through interaction of staff with inmates. By eliminating these barriers, the potential for good staff/inmate relations is magnified many times and most problems are neutralized before they get out-of-hand as staff, performing proactively and not reactively, mix and talk with inmates, feel the pulse of the institution, and intervene in potential problems before they become serious. *It has been said that the difference between observation and supervision is a wall.*

Except, perhaps, for maximum security institutions, standard construction techniques can be used for most buildings, such as the dining and food preparation areas, educational facilities, visiting rooms, and industrial area. Some buildings or areas, however, require more secure construction. These include the entrance structure, control center, armory, locksmith shop, cashier's office, mail room, information management office, pharmacy, canteen, admissions and discharge holding rooms, medical inpatient area, and all housing structures. While most construction within the interior of these areas can be done with standard materials and systems, the envelope surrounding these areas must be secure. Doors, locks, and other hardware must provide equivalent security. The methods of constructing these secure envelopes varies; a discussion of security construction for walls, ceilings, and floors follows.

Walls. Typically, either concrete or masonry is used for secure wall construction. If concrete is chosen, the standard steel reinforcing used with pre-cast or cast-in-place concrete is usually sufficient.

Masonry walls require special attention to attain appropriate security qualities. About the only practical masonry construction that can be made secure is constructed of concrete block, used alone or "faced" with other materials such as brick, stone, or wood.

Concrete block for secure walls should be 8 inches thick. While blocks 6 inches thick may be satisfactory in some instances if needed for reasons other than security, they are more difficult to make secure. To be secure, walls should be reinforced with ½-inch round steel reinforcing bars placed at 8 inches on center, both vertically and horizontally. Each vertical cell and each horizontal course is reinforced to create an 8-by 8-inch steel grid. Steel bars should overlap a minimum of 18 inches and end bars should be adequately anchored to adjoining walls, floors, and ceilings to provide continuity of the security grid system. In addition, 3,000 pounds-per-square-inch concrete grout must be used to completely fill each concrete block cell. Masonry walls around the control room and armory should be con-

Some buildings or areas, however, require more secure construction. These include the entrance structure, control center, armory, locksmith shop, cashier's office, mail room, information management office, pharmacy, canteen, admissions and discharge holding rooms, medical in-patient area, and all housing structures. While most construction within the interior of these areas can be done with standard materials and systems, the envelope surrounding these areas must be secure.

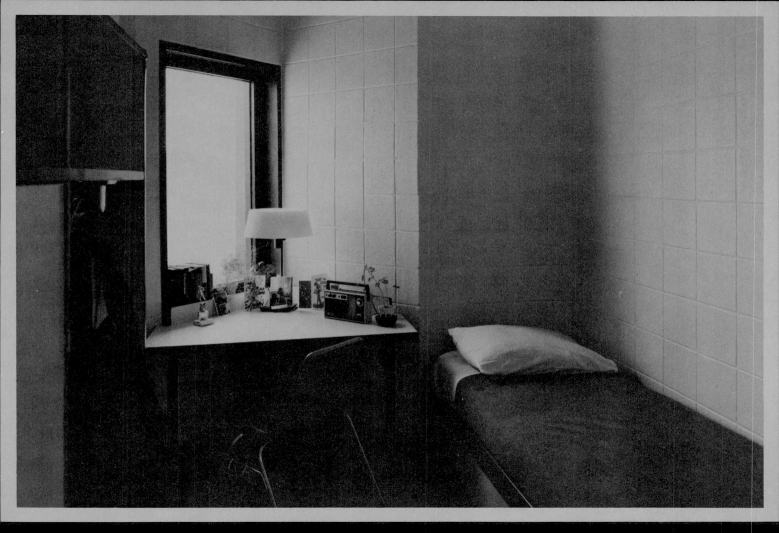

While the envelope of the housing structure

structed with concrete block at least 8 inches thick and include the grouted steel bar grid. While doors into the control room and armory should be made of 12-gauge steel, with frames made of 10-gauge steel filled with concrete, most other secure doors can be made of 14-gauge steel with 12-gauge concrete-filled steel frames.

Intensive supervision of the secure masonry construction is necessary during the construction period to ensure that no steel bars are omitted by workmen. One method used in the past to ensure compliance has been to x-ray the walls periodically and randomly. The general contractor and the masonry subcontractor should be informed at the outset of any such plans.

It is especially important that all security walls extend all the way to a secure ceiling and that they be appropriately anchored. Particular attention must be paid whenever non-secure "drop" ceilings are used; it is not uncommon for designers or contractors to erroneously terminate secure walls a few inches above a non-secure ceiling system, thus creating potential access across secure barriers above the ceiling line.

Openings in secure walls, ceilings, and floors should not exceed 8 by 8 inches, or 5 inches in width if the length is longer than 8 inches, unless they are secured to prevent passage by inmates. Wall openings exceeding these dimensions require security doors, special security windows, or secure steel bar grids such as those placed in openings for heating and cooling ductwork.

Except for maximum security institutions, nearly all interior walls of a secure structure or area can be built with standard materials, although adequate consideration should be given to durability. Non-secure concrete block walls are used extensively throughout the interior in most facilities and have proven satisfactory, especially when painted with lively color schemes including, perhaps, "super graphics" in bold

Non-secure concrete block walls are used extensively throughout the interior in most facilities and have proven satisfactory, especially when painted with lively color schemes including super graphics.

colors for area or room designations or as directional guides. While some authorities believe the interior walls of individual inmate rooms or cells must be securely constructed, others have found such measures unnecessary as long as housing units are managed by well-trained staff who provide good control and supervision and establish sound, professional rapport with the inmates. Similarly, individual doors and locking systems need not be as heavy-duty as those found in traditional facilities, thus creating further substantial savings in dollars. There are numerous examples of successful designs using non-secure interior walls, doors made of 16-gauge steel and frames made of 14-gauge concrete-reinforced steel, with moderate-duty locks, rather than heavy-duty doors and prison locks or traditional institutional doors and barred grilles.

Ceiling and Floors. Concrete ceilings and floors constructed to hold the weight of the structure and contents are usually sufficiently reinforced to meet security requirements. If metal roof decks are used, they should have a non-lightweight concrete topping.

Any openings for ducts or other purposes that are larger than the dimensions previously discussed must be fitted with suitable steel bar grids or equally effective barriers.

Windows. Windows contribute to the security of an institution by providing better vision and enhancing surveillance. They also help normalize the general atmosphere of a facility by making it more "open" and humane.

Windows are the weakest security point in a wall. Traditionally, most windows within a correctional facility were usually specified to be "security-type." Due in part to improvements in perimeter security systems, fewer areas today require expensive security windows. The education and recreation facilities, for example, generally do not need a secure envelope. Areas that do require security windows include the housing units, the control center, spaces where inmates are not allowed access such as the pharmacy, and, in general, any area where windows comprise part of the security perimeter or part of a secure envelope within a building.

Three options are available for areas that require secure windows: specially manufactured security windows and frames; secure window glazing, such as polycarbonate plastic alone or glass combined with polycarbonate plastic; and concrete or steel sections placed in the clear openings to preclude passage by inmates. The last method is the least expensive and uses standard commercial windows placed within a window opening of any height or length. The clear "secure" opening must not exceed 5 inches. To gain a better view and more light, wider openings can be provided, but the maximum security clearance is maintained by placing heavy-duty concrete or tubular steel sections at appropriate intervals within the opening. If steel tubes are used, they are filled with concrete for added strength and resistance and placed on either the inside or the outside of the windows. If concrete is used, the edges must be protected with steel edging.

It is important to note that no known security window system, traditional or contemporary, is escape-proof. Windows with steel bars or security steel grilles can be breached

The use of plastic products for secure glazing has been growing in recent years. These new glazings enable designers to incorporate windows in their designs that create more pleasing environments for both staff and inmates.

with new devices such as a small, flexible saw made of steel wire coated with an abrasive. These saws are easily smuggled into institutions where, because of their small mass, they are often undetected even when passed through metal detectors. Similarly, bar spreaders, which are fairly easy for inmates to fabricate, can quickly render steel grillwork ineffective.

The use of plastic products for secure glazing has been growing in recent years. These new glazings enable designers to incorporate windows in their designs that create more pleasing environments for both staff and inmates. Generally, polycarbonate plastic used alone for glazing should be 3/8-inch thick. Polycarbonate, however, has some disadvantages. Even with a protective coating, it is subject to scratching and surface weathering. It also bends considerably and can be sawed easily. Since these qualities are unsatisfactory in most areas requiring security glazing, new products have been developed that have glass laminated onto both sides of a layer of polycarbonate plastic. While considerably more expensive, this combination of materials is much stiffer, wears well

and is not as easily sawed. Even if the glass is fractured, much of it continues to adhere to the laminating material, thus retaining its resistance to sawing. There are many potential combinations of material thicknesses. The most cost-effective combination appears to be ¼-inch polycarbonate plastic laminated between two layers of 1/8-inch tempered glass. A less expensive option that wears well, but does not resist sawing as well, is a product that has a 1/8-inch tempered glass placed on both sides of a 3/8-inch sheet of polycarbonate, with an air gap between each layer of glass and the sheet of polycarbonate. If the glass is broken, the polycarbonate is exposed, making it vulnerable to sawing. Although this product costs less than the glass-laminated polycarbonate, it is also easier to penetrate.

Bullet-resistant laminated glass (multiple layers of glass bound together by laminating vinyl) is not a substitute for glass-laminated polycarbonate. While bullet-resistant laminated glass is appropriate when only bullet-resistance is required, this type of glass can be broken easily with makeshift implements, enabling inmates to enter a secure area in a mat-

ter of seconds. Glass-laminated polycarbonate, on the other hand, while not as bullet-resistant, is much more resistant to penetration. If the primary intent is to prevent inmates from entering an area, glass-laminated polycarbonate should be used.

Regardless of the security glazing, very careful attention must be given to the strength of the window frame, the anchorage of the frame into the wall, and the adequacy of the removable portions (stops), together with their fasteners. The stops must be located on the side of the window least accessible to inmates. For example, they should be placed on the outside of windows in inmate rooms, but on the inside of the windows in the control center.

Given enough time, any secure window system can be breached. The question is whether the chosen system provides adequate time for staff to react in the event of an attempted breakthrough. Glass-laminated polycarbonate has served well by this measure, but, as with any security system throughout a correctional facility, sound operational procedures are a prerequisite to its success.

The control center is the "nerve center" for the entire facility. Control center activities include observing and controlling the institution's entrance and exit traffic, recording all inmate counts, monitoring fire and security alarm systems, operating central communication systems, issuing and maintaining an inventory of institution keys, operating electrically controlled doors, monitoring the perimeter, and operating telephone equipment. Each of these activities has a critical impact on the institution's orderly and secure operation.

The control center operation integrates all internal and external security communication networks. It must be secure from outside assault and at the same time afford good visibility of the areas it is designed to monitor. Its size is determined largely by the type and amount of equipment used and the extent of the duties assigned to the staff in this area. The equipment should be organized so that one person can monitor and operate it easily.

Since a large amount of equipment is required, display panels and annunciation equipment are minia-

CONTROL CENTER

turized and located in the control center, while supporting electronic equipment is located in a nearby equipment room. The control center should have raised-access flooring like that used in a computer room to facilitate wiring and maintenance of the equipment. Because the center is a crucial and highly specialized 24-hour operation, a separate heating and cooling system should be provided to ensure uninterrupted climate control.

All control center activities are under the supervision of the chief of security, and the center is staffed 24 hours a day, seven days a week, by at least one staff member. During periods of peak activity, such as inmate counts and staff shift changes, additional security officers are often assigned to this area. To alleviate the heavy daytime work load, incoming telephone calls to the institution are often answered by a receptionist stationed in the front entrance building (see "Entrances" later in this chapter). At night, when a receptionist is not needed at this post, incoming calls are switched to the control center.

The control center is often a part of the administration building and is preferably located about 50 feet from the front pedestrian sally port so that staff assigned to the control center can observe the entrance area. Closed circuit television in the control center allows close visual coverage of both the pedestrian and vehicular sally ports (see "Entrances"). The control center usually occupies about 450 square feet and uses large amounts of secure glazing to ensure clear sight lines to the front entrance and permit

The control center is the "nerve center" for the entire facility. Control center activities include observing and controlling the institution's entrance and exit traffic, recording all inmate counts, monitoring fire and security alarm systems, operating central communication systems, issuing and maintaining an inventory of institution keys, operating electrically controlled doors, monitoring the perimeter, and operating telephone equipment. Each of these activities has a critical impact on the institution's orderly and secure operation.

The control center (above) is often a part of the administration building. Preferably, it is located about 50 feet from the front pedestrian sally port. Large amounts of secure glazing are used to ensure clear sight lines both to the front entrance and into the compound. (Right) It is staffed 24 hours a day, seven days a week by at least one staff member. Additional security staff are often assigned to this area during peak periods of activity.

observation of people passing from the sally port to various buildings. Its location should provide a view of as much of the main compound as possible, adding to the control center officer's ability to casually survey general inmate activity and circulation. Its location should also permit observation of entrances to the visiting, admissions/discharge, and administration facilities.

Because the officer must remain inside the control center at all times, a toilet and janitor's closet should be provided inside the secure envelope of the control center complex. Storage space is provided in the control center for certain emergency equipment, including riot sticks, helmets, shields, first aid kits, and perhaps tear gas.

To prevent unauthorized access, a small sally port provides entrance security into the complex. The outer door should be operated electrically by the control center officer, precluding staff outside the control center from opening the door. The inner door should be operated manually so that the control center officer must go to the sally port and visually verify the identity of persons before admit-

To prevent unauthorized access, a small sally port provides entrance security into the control center. The outer door should be operated electronically while the inner door should be operated manually so that control center staff must visually verify the identity of persons before admission.

ting them into the control center. An emergency key to the center should be kept outside the institution's secure perimeter so that the control center can be opened if the officer is suddenly incapacitated.

A room of about 400 square feet is needed to house the equipment required to operate the control center, including telephone and alarm switching equipment, battery back ups, and computers. The equipment room should be adjacent to, or one floor below or above, the control center. Locating it below the control center normally provides the easiest access for the necessary electrical wiring. It is advisable to provide a sally port entrance to this room. If the equipment room is adjacent to the control center, the sally port to the control center can serve as a secure entrance for both spaces; if the room is below or above the control center, a second sally port is recommended, as is closed circuit television monitoring of this entrance.

The entire envelope surrounding this complex—control center, toilet, janitor's closet, sally port, and electronic equipment room—should be of secure construction to prevent

unauthorized admittance. The inner walls, such as those between the janitor's closet and the control center, do not require security construction.

Communication Devices

Closed Circuit Television. The use of closed circuit television (CCTV) as a security tool is very cost-

effective for many applications. It is an excellent device for monitoring fence lines, roof tops, tunnels, and corridors and aids in the identification of people passing through a sally port. Some types of CCTV cameras even detect motion in their field of view and alert the control center if someone is in an unauthorized area.

CCTV should not be used to

Closed circuit television is an excellent device for monitoring fence lines, roof tops, tunnels, and corridors. It aids in identification of people passing through a sally port. However, it should not be used to monitor inmates in their regular activities.

monitor inmates in their regular duties and functions. There is no electronic substitute for the valuable personal interaction between inmates and staff. In institutions where every move is monitored with CCTV, inmates are more alienated and have poorer perceptions of themselves, thus diminishing attitudes usually necessary for self-improvement.

Paging System. Paging systems allow the control center officer or other designated staff members to make general announcements throughout the institution, summon individuals, and alert staff about emergencies. Because institution-wide paging causes unnecessary disruptions in areas unaffected by specific announcements, zone paging is recommended. A listen-in/talk-back function adds the capability to monitor a specific location or to conduct a conversation.

Two-Way Radios. A combination of portable or car radios, and a base station provides instantaneous two-way communications over an assigned radio frequency. The power output of the base station and the portable radio sets should be sufficient to establish a clear communications link between sets anywhere

near the institution, including a clear link between the base station and the farthest distance staff are expected to travel during an escape search.

Before operating on any radio frequency, authorization must be obtained from the Federal Communications Commission.

Institution staff usually pick up portable radios at the control center and return them for storage and recharging at the end of their work shift. An adequate pass-through system must be installed in the front wall

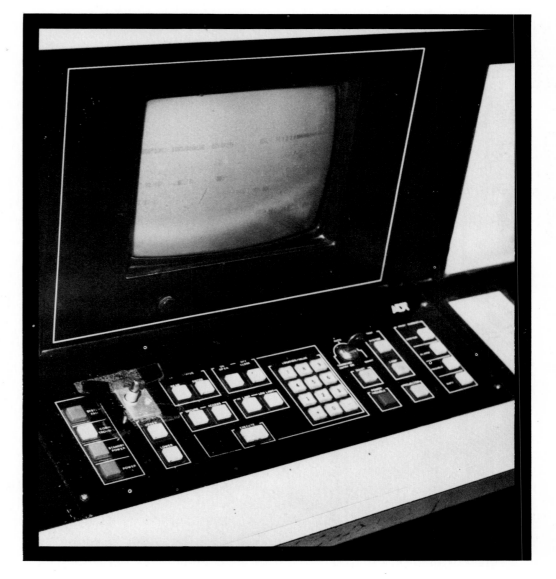

Sophisticated electronic systems such as two-way radios, paging devices, intrusion alarm networks, body alarms, and advanced telephone communications are important tools in providing security while at the same time minimizing the atmosphere of surveillance.

of the control center to allow the officer to issue and receive radios.

Staff Body Alarms. Alarms are provided to selected staff to enable them to summon assistance in an emergency. These alarms are worn on the body and transmit a signal to the control center when activated.

Two basic types of body alarms are currently available. One is an ultrasonic system that transmits an inaudible signal to receivers spaced every 30 linear feet throughout the institution. The receivers are connected to the control center and when the ultrasonic signal is picked up by a receiver, an alarm is sounded in the control center identifying the location of the alarm.

The second type of body alarm operates on a radio frequency. This alarm produces a tone-coded FM signal that identifies which body alarm has been activated. An even more effective, but more costly, variation of this alarm is equipped with an audio feature that, when activated, enables the control room officer to hear the ambient sounds near the activated instrument for a 10-second period. The purpose is to communicate to the control center officer both the nature and location of the problem.

Telephone Equipment. Historically, telephone equipment in correctional facilities has consisted of two systems, one operating inside the institution and a separate system operating outside the institution. The outside system was normally provided by the local telephone company and was comparable to the systems provided to most businesses. Telephone instruments with access to the outside system were located in secure areas, and inmates were restricted from using them.

The inside telephone system is specifically designated for correctional facilities and is considered an integral part of the institution's security system. Special features include watch call, emergency alert, no-dial alarm, and executive right-of-way. The watch call feature enables each officer making an inmate count to call a special number; these calls "stack" onto an open line in the control center for continuous and simultaneous communication until the count clears. The emergency alert feature, also initiated by dialing a special number, activates an emergency network that simultaneously rings pre-designated phones such as those in the control center, CEO's office, and the chief of security's office. The no-dial alarm is activated when a handset is removed from its base instrument for at least 15 seconds prior to dialing; this alarm also indicates the location of the instrument being dialed. The executive right-of-way feature allows staff at certain phones, such as those in the CEO's office or the control center, to interrupt calls if lines are busy, thus enabling an emergency call to be completed immediately.

It is recommended that planners consider a single solid-state telephone system that combines the security features of the inside telephone system with the flexibility of the outside system. Such a system is now being marketed and has proved successful. This new system resolves many of the installation, interface, operational, and maintenance problems associated with the traditional dual system.

A battery-operated backup system for operating telephones must be provided for maintaining communications in case of an interruption in the institution's electrical supply.

It is recommended that planners consider a single solid-state telephone system that combines the security features of the inside telephone system with the flexibility of the outside system. Such a system is now being marketed and has proved successful. This new system resolves many of the installation, interface, operational, and maintenance problems associated with the traditional dual system.

To provide good surveillance, adequate "buffer zones" are required both inside and outside the secure compound. As a rule, the minimum distance between the outer perimeter fence and the institution's property lines should be 300 feet. Up to 600 feet is preferred, if possible, and greater distances may be necessary whenever facilities such as the warehouse, fire station, power plant or sewage treatment plant are located outside the fence. If natural barriers such as mountains or rivers are nearby, security beyond the compound perimeter can often be enhanced by careful siting relative to these barriers (see Chapter I, "Site Selection and Acquisition").

For good surveillance of the perimeter zone inside the compound, the desired minimum distance between buildings and the inner perimeter is 150 feet of unobstructed space, although some authorities reduce the minimum to 100 feet. Shorter distances may be permissible if local conditions justify a smaller clearance, the implications are studied carefully, and local authorities are aware of the implications. One exception to this rule is the building where the control

COMPOUND PERIMETER

center is located, which is frequently the administration building, as the desired maximum distance between the main entrance sally port and the control center is 50 feet.

Contemporary medium security institutions are usually surrounded by two chain link fences, a minimum of 12 feet high and sufficiently distant from buildings and recreation fields to create an open area near the fence

that is "off limits" to inmates. Preferably, openings in the fences occur at only two points: the pedestrian sally port at the main entrance, and the vehicular sally port, which is usually located at the side or rear of the institution.

At some existing institutions, the administration building serves as part of the perimeter. This feature should be avoided because a large building at the fence line blocks vision and creates unnecessary hiding places near the fence. Another tradition, and one practiced at most institutions, has been to locate the administration building in front of the perimeter security line, thus placing most administrative personnel, including the chief executive officer and other top staff, outside the security zone of the institution. It is recommended that all administrative staff be located inside the institution, in order to be more accessible to other personnel and closer to inmate programs and activities. Closer physical contact with these programs and activities will better ensure that policies and procedures are followed and will enable top staff to better sense the pulse and emotional climate of the institution.

The two perimeter fences should be placed 20 to 30 feet apart. This distance prevents potential escapees from easily jumping to the second fence if they have reached the top of the first one, or from easily straddling the fences with devices such as ladders. It also provides adequate space to place rolls of "security wire" between the fences while leaving a pathway to apprehend potential escapees. This type of security wire is a recently developed barbed wire, composed of razor-sharp stainless steel points that act more like fish hooks than barbs, which further entangles anyone caught in it who tries to escape. Both fences should be equipped with this security wire. The configuration at the outer fence, with more wire at the bottom of the fence than at the top, inhibits potential escapees from gaining access to the fence.

The fence system should surround the entire institution. As a general rule, it should not be curved because a curved fence produces more blind spots, making it more difficult to patrol than straight-line fence segments, which create few, if any,

blind spots. In addition, certain types of electronic perimeter detection systems require straight fence lines. Acute angles are not advisable because they are easier to climb.

The fence's wire fabric should be attached on the side of the fence facing the institution, so that fence posts and rails are located on the outside and cannot be used for climbing. Whenever fence-mounted electronic intrusion sensors are used, the fabric should be very tightly stretched to prevent wind vibration.

In higher-security institutions, underground barriers are sometimes placed under the inner fence to inhibit tunneling. Concrete grade beams or metal barriers serve this purpose. Another alternative is to use underground electronic sensors to detect the presence of people between the two fences. These sensors have been used successfully in all but the coldest climates and are intended to detect tunneling. Maximum security institutions, however, may require subsoil barriers as well as underground detection systems.

Some type of an electronic perimeter detection system is recommended for secure correctional facilities.

When properly designed, installed, and operated, a perimeter system immediately alerts staff to a breach of the perimeter. Because conditions vary from site to site, no single system is best for all situations. Options include microwave, infrared, electric field, seismic, and fence disturbance systems, but the proper selection depends on multiple factors, including topography, vegetation, wildlife, weather, soil conditions, background noise, and staff response time. The job of the design engineer is to find the best match of individual system characteristics with local conditions.

During the 1970s, numerous misapplications of electronic technology occurred, largely because of the eagerness of both clients and vendors, all of whom genuinely believed in the viability of technologies not yet broadly tested in the field of corrections. In addition, a frequent problem in the early deployment of electronic security systems was the lack of technical specialists who could maintain the systems on a daily basis, or at least on very short notice. The importance of this point should not be overlooked. It is better to forego state-of-

A reliable perimeter security system allows inside operations to be more relaxed, with less need for constant observation of the inmate's every movement and a resulting reduction in both inmate and staff tensions.

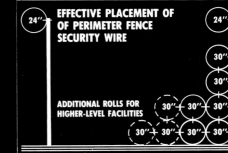

**EFFECTIVE PLACEMENT OF
OF PERIMETER FENCE
SECURITY WIRE**

24″   24″

30″

30″

**ADDITIONAL ROLLS FOR
HIGHER-LEVEL FACILITIES**   30″ 30″ 30″

30″ 30″ 30″ 30″

the-art electronic technology unless there is a commitment to adequate maintenance of the system, including the capability for quick responsiveness in the event of malfunctions.

Fortunately, experience and research has led to a better understanding about how to use electronic perimeter detection systems satisfactorily. One source of information is the *Intrusion Detection Systems Handbook,* a publication of the Sandia Laboratories, Albuquerque, New Mexico. This publication is updated periodically and presents an evaluation of various electronic systems based on extensive research under varying conditions.

Twenty-four hour surveillance of the outside perimeter fence is generally provided for both medium and higher security institutions through either watch towers or mobile vehicular patrols. Watch towers provide a good view of the perimeter but are very expensive to construct and operate. A typical institution requires four to six watch towers. Each tower that employs 24-hour tower coverage requires over five staff to provide coverage when vacation, sick leave, and relief time are considered. They

are reasonably secure from assault from the ground and safe for weapons storage, but officers in towers must rely primarily on the threat of gunfire to deter escapes. Mobile patrols, on the other hand, can intercept and apprehend escapees without using gunfire. Moreover, it is believed that the relatively boring job of watch tower duty renders tower personnel less alert and responsive, compared to those on mobile patrol duty.

When used, watch towers must be securely constructed and designed for maximum visibility in all directions. Windows must be designed to open quickly so that weapons can be fired through them. Storage space for weapons and ammunition is included in the tower cabs. Search lights are usually affixed to the tops of towers. Communications devices that permit

continuous contact with other towers, patrols, and the control center are also needed. If meals are not brought to the officer, a small refrigerator is usually provided for food storage. Toilet facilities must be included and designed so that a tower officer using the facilities can still see outside and along the fence lines. These provisions make towers very costly to construct.

Generally, towers are located outside truncated fence corners to provide clear sight lines between the fences in both directions. Additional towers may be needed because of the facility's configuration or to maintain a maximum distance between towers of 600 feet. Any greater distances between towers render them virtually useless for accurate gunfire and useful only for observation. To ensure good sight lines, tower floors should be a

A perimeter surveillance system now in growing use is the mobile patrol. The savings in staff for a typical institution that uses mobile patrols rather than watch towers range from 12 to 18 staff years—a savings of $300,000 to $500,000 per year.

minimum of 30 feet above the ground level at the adjacent fence line. If a perimeter lighting system is used, the design should provide for the eye level of the tower officer to be above the level of the lights.

The primary alternative perimeter surveillance system, now in growing use, is mobile patrols. Typically, two mobile patrol vehicles, each manned by one officer, survey the perimeter during active program hours. During sleeping hours, only one patrol vehicle is usually active since inmates are locked in their housing units and the probability of escape attempts is substantially reduced. The savings in staff for a typical institution that uses the mobile patrol system rather than the watch tower system ranges from 12 to 18 staff years. In 1983 dollars, this savings could amount to $300,000 to $500,000 a year, considering both salaries and fringe benefits.

Each mobile patrol vehicle is equipped with a continuously active two-way radio in order to stay in constant contact with the control center officer and other mobile patrols, including any foot patrols. The vehicle as well as the control center is equipped with a monitor that visually reflects the site plan of the institution, including the perimeter fence. The perimeter is divided into zones. If a zone is violated, electronic sensors simultaneously alert the patrol and control center officers by an audible tone and a visual alarm on the monitor that indicates which zone has been violated. The patrol car officer rushes to investigate that area and takes appropriate action.

Effective perimeter security also requires a good exterior lighting system. The traditional method is to place lights at 100-foot intervals along the entire perimeter, with additional lights placed at building locations both inside and outside the fence and at other locations around the compound. In recent years, "high-mast" lighting systems have become popular. Each fixture in these systems illuminates a very large area and provides a minimum of one-half foot candle power at ground level. By using only a few high-mast light poles— usually five to eight, each 100 to 120 feet tall—the entire compound and perimeter can be adequately lighted with considerable savings in both capital and operating costs. If half of the lamps in each fixture are sodium vapor-type and the other half metal halide-type, the combination provides an economical system and a satisfactory quality of light. The lights on each high-mast pole should be subdivided into two groups and operated from the control room. This feature allows the control room officer to reduce the light level during the midnight-to-dawn period, when inmates are locked in their housing units, and produces further savings in operating expenses.

Mobile patrols are usually equipped with a two-way radio plus an electronic site plan of the institution that alerts the patrol officer to the zone where the perimeter is violated.

Most secure correctional institutions have a main or "front" entrance for pedestrian traffic and a side or "rear" entrance that is used primarily for vehicles.

Front Entrance. The entrance building is the principal entry and exit point for all pedestrians, inmates, staff, visitors, volunteers, and vendors. To a large degree, first impressions influence attitudes about the program throughout the institution. The entrance design should convey a business-like and congenial atmosphere that supports the public's perception of a well-administered and professional program.

It is recommended that the main entrance be located in a structure separate from the main buildings and comprise a waiting area, reception station, armory, locksmith shop, and sally port. This structure can be relatively small and its walls should have considerable amounts of glazing to provide good visibility for surveillance. It should be situated directly in the path of the perimeter fence system between the parking lot and the control center, thus becoming an integral part of the perimeter security.

ENTRANCES

Security wire and electronic detection devices are affixed to the roof and sides of the building. A clear zone of about 50 feet between this building and the control center, which is usually located with the administration building, gives good visibility from the control center to and around the front entrance building.

An area with a minimum of 800 square feet should be provided in the entrance building for visitors awaiting clearance to enter the institution. All visitors to an institution are screened by a walk-through metal detector. Those who fail to "clear" a walk-through detector can be subjected to closer screening with a hand-held detector. Failure to pass the hand-held detector would require the individual to submit to a more thorough body search before being allowed to enter the institution.

On occasion, designers have promoted the integration of metal detectors into the general architectural features in a way that hides these sometimes unsightly detectors from view. While this approach may be more aesthetic, such improvements should not produce a system so hidden or unobtrusive that people being screened are unaware of it. Part of the effectiveness of a metal detection device is the certain knowledge that such a system is being used.

All packages entering the facility should be opened and inspected. (Package x-ray machines are sometimes used for inspections, but are not effective for detecting drugs and non-metallic weapons.) Lockers, including special security lockers for law enforcement officers' weapons, are provided for storing items that are not allowed in the institution. A

To a large degree, first impressions influence attitudes about the program throughout the institution. The entrance design should convey a business-like and congenial atmosphere that supports the public's perception of a well-administered and professional program.

The entrance building should have an area for visitors awaiting clearance to enter the institution. A walk-through metal detector and storage lockers for items not allowed inside should be provided.

reception station is provided where a receptionist "clears" visitors. This station, occupying about 50 square feet, is sometimes staffed during daytime hours by a receptionist who answers the telephone for the entire institution, relieving the control center of this task. When the receptionist is not on duty, calls are switched to the control center where staff can answer the telephone.

Both a men's and a women's rest room should be located off of the waiting area for use by the public and staff; fixtures for handicapped persons must be provided. A janitor's closet should also be located adjacent to the waiting area.

The entrance into the secure area of the institution, is through a 150-square-foot sally port that is integrated into the entrance building. A sally port is a very secure enclosure with two electrically operated doors. Its operation is similar to an "air lock," with only one door allowed open at any one time. The control center officer operates the sally port doors by remote control. The front sally port should be clearly visible from the control center and not more than 50 feet away. When a person has

The sally port doors are controlled electronically by the control room officer. Only one door can be opened at a time.

The sally port should be located between the reception officer's station and the control center. In this way, both officers have a clear view of everyone entering and leaving the institution through the main entrance.

entered the sally port, the control center officer should conduct a final check by closed circuit television to ensure that the proper person is in the sally port.

Particular attention must be given to the construction of the entire sally port envelope to ensure adequate security. In addition, certain walls and doors should contain large amounts of security glazing to promote optimum visibility by staff, especially the control room officer.

Sometimes an administration building is located so that it, rather than the entrance structure, becomes part of the perimeter security line. The size and mass of the administration building, however, precludes clear sight lines on either one side of the fence or the other. In addition, the large roof area becomes a potential weak zone in the perimeter system.

Rear Entrance. The rear or side entrance, commonly called the vehicular sally port, is used primarily for allowing service or delivery vehicles into the secure area of the institution. It is an integral part of the perimeter fence system, and there should be a clear zone between this sally port and

other institution buildings to maintain good surveillance. The electrically operated sally port gates are controlled from the control center or a nearby tower whenever towers are used. Radio, telephone, and closed circuit television are used to coordinate this activity. (Officers stationed within a sally port should never operate the gates. If officers have this responsibility, inmates may overtake them, open the sally port, and escape.)

After the vehicle enters the sally port and the gate is closed, the sally port officer screens the driver and passengers and searches the vehicle. If everything is satisfactory, the officer radios the control center to open the second gate. The control center officer monitors the sally port area through closed-circuit television to ensure that the sally port officer is not giving approval while under duress.

All vehicles and their contents should be inspected to ensure that neither contraband nor unauthorized inmates are being transported through the sally port. Space may be needed within the sally port to hold vehicles or store materials that are not inspected, such as sealed cartons

from an industrial operation. Such items usually remain in the sally port overnight, or until at least one official inmate census has been completed, to ensure that no inmate is trying to escape by hiding in the vehicles or cargo.

Pedestrian gates are also incorporated into the vehicular sally port. These are used by inmates who are on work details outside the institution and by staff who have business in facilities located outside the compound but close to the vehicular sally

The entrance building (left) is an integral part of the secure perimeter. Security wire and electronic detection devices (right) are affixed to the roof and sides of the building.

port. All persons must be identified and carefully screened before entrance or exit.

While open for operation, the vehicular entrance is staffed by at least one full-time security officer stationed within the sally port. Frequently, two officers are needed during periods of heavy traffic. Such assistance is often provided by officers who would otherwise be engaged in escort, perimeter patrol, or tower coverage duties. A small weather shelter should be provided inside the sally port to serve as an officer's station.

The vehicular sally port is usually constructed of the same material as the perimeter fence and should enclose about 2,800 square feet. This area is large enough to hold two trucks, one entering the institution and one being held or detained. Removable bollards, or metal posts, should be placed in front of the gates to deter escape attempts by inmates who might commandeer a vehicle and try to crash through the gates. The sally port should protrude into the compound, not outward, so that the view along the outside perimeter fence line remains unobstructed.

Both the front and rear entrance sally ports should have emergency mechanical override keys. The keys should be kept in an area outside the secure zone of the institution that is accessible only to authorized persons. They should not be kept in the control center, since this area could conceivably be surrounded by inmates during a major disturbance, jeopardizing staff's access to the keys. Keyways on the doors or gates of the sally ports should be placed only on the outward-facing sides, thus preventing inmates inside the institution from gaining access to them.

The rear or vehicle sally port also has two gates that are electronically operated from the control center or a nearby tower—never by the sally port officer. After the officer screens the vehicle and driver, he notifies the control center to open the gate.

Armory

Virtually all secure correctional institutions require space for storing firearms, ammunition, and other security equipment. This area, usually known as the armory, must be located so that it is not accessible to inmates. The entrance to the armory should be outside the institution's perimeter security. The armory can be located with any "outside" structure; however, it is usually best to include it as part of the front entrance structure because this location is easily accessible to staff in emergencies. Because they have similar security requirements, the armory and locksmith shop are sometimes located in the same area. The materials used to construct the armory must provide for maximum security and safety (see "Building Security").

An armory of about 150 square feet is normally sufficient for the storage, cleaning, and maintenance of weapons and equipment. The room should be equipped with metal storage shelving and an issue window sized to issue all weapons safely. The armory also should be climate-con-

ARMORY AND LOCKSMITH SHOP

trolled to preserve the chemicals and ammunition in storage.

The armory is supervised by a security officer who is specially trained in handling and maintaining weapons. Additional officers are assigned to assist in the armory during emergencies.

Locksmith Shop

The locksmith's primary responsibility is to keep all institutional locking devices in good operating condition. The shop provides key cutting, lock maintenance and repair, and storage of supplies and equipment. While additional duties are sometimes assigned to the locksmith, administrators should ensure that extra duties do not interfere with the locksmith's principal role.

Like the armory, the locksmith shop must be inaccessible to inmates. The shop should contain about 200 square feet and must be securely constructed. While it can be located with other outside buildings, it is recommended that the shop be positioned as part of the entrance structure.

The armory is a secure, climate-controlled space of about 150 square feet for the storage, cleaning, and maintenance of weapons and equipment.

The locksmith shop (left) provides key cutting, lock maintenance and repair, and storage of supplies and equipment. Both the locksmith shop and the armory should be located outside the secure perimeter, preferably as part of the entrance building. The armory (above) has an issue window for the safe issuance of weapons.

Proper location of the institution's roads and parking area facilitates good traffic control and enhances perimeter surveillance. Preferably, all vehicles, including commercial trucks and staff and visitors' cars, should enter the property by the same road. The route for commercial trucks should diverge from the automobile route before reaching the staff and visitors' parking lot and proceed directly to the vehicular sally port.

The parking area for staff and visitors should be located near the front entrance, sufficiently away from the perimeter fence so that perimeter surveillance is not hindered. The area should be well-lighted because of the 24-hour work schedule, and the number of spaces assigned to staff parking should be adequate for accommodating the two sets of staff present during shift changes. The space needed for visitor parking will depend on such factors as inmates' proximity to relatives, their marital status, visiting rules, and the availability of public transportation. Ordinarily, about 250 parking spaces are needed for both staff and visitors at a 500-bed facility.

ROADS AND PARKING

A road encircling the compound perimeter is needed if mobile perimeter patrols are used. The road should be paved with an all-weather surface, as should the entrance road and parking lot. The perimeter security road should contain at least three "turn-arounds" so that patrol vehicles can reverse their direction quickly. This road is also used by any foot patrols thay may be needed during unusual weather conditions such as dense fog.

The perimeter security road should run parallel to the fence for optimum visual surveillance of the perimeter, although some deviations from this course may be necessary because of terrain or to gain a better vantage point for viewing the perimeter. The parking lot should be located outside the perimeter road to maintain open views to the fence.

The preferred distance from the perimeter security road to the perimeter fence is 40 to 50 feet. In no case should the distance be less than 20 feet or more than 75 feet since visual surveillance is impaired beyond either extreme. Ideally, there should be at least 300 feet between the perimeter road and the facility's property line; the first 50 feet from the perimeter road should be totally cleared of trees or other obstacles.

Firetrucks and maintenance and delivery vehicles owned by the institution need access to all buildings inside the perimeter. Special sidewalks should be designed to provide trucks or emergency vehicles with access to all buildings, unless the soil conditions are such that heavy vehicles can drive over the terrain regardless of weather.

The preferred distance from the perimeter security road to the perimeter fence is 40 to 50 feet. In no case should the distance be less than 20 feet or more than 75 feet since visual surveillance is impaired beyond either extreme.

Ramps and other provisions for the handicapped must be considered in the design of the facility, especially in those areas where the public has frequent access such as the visiting rooms and administrative offices.

APPENDIXES

A number of methods can be used to determine personnel needs. The guidelines given below are those developed by the Federal Bureau of Prisons and currently in force in federal institutions. The guidelines are based on a research design that incorporated the opinions and experiences of all federal managers of functional correctional programs while taking into account the existing limitations on available resources. They are presented as a reference point from which individual correctional managers can analyze their unique staffing needs and develop staffing guidelines tailored to their own particular institutions and resource capabilities.

To develop its staffing guidelines, the Bureau appointed a special task force that solicited the opinions of all functional program managers. Each manager was asked to submit a proposed staffing pattern based on a realistic assessment of the number of staff needed to operate the program effectively. The number of positions requested had to be justified on the basis of existing standards, needs assessments, and other supporting documentation. In addition, managers were cautioned to neither overstate nor understate their needs, but to formulate proposals within the framework of limited public resources. In short, the Bureau was seeking practical judgments on what it takes to run an effective program rather than statements of optimum or minimum staff size.

Once the guidelines were established, they were compared with existing staffing patterns in state correctional systems. The comparison revealed that about half of the states had a higher staff-to-inmate ratio and about half had a lower ratio. The widest variations occurred within security force staffing patterns. This is probably due to two factors: 1) differences in the use of watch towers versus mobile patrols for perimeter security, and 2) the varying use of decentralized inmate management programs, which allow some correctional officer positions to be converted to positions for correctional counselors, caseworkers, or team managers.

The guidelines are presented in the form of tables that indicate how to determine and apply the appropriate guideline for each program area. The following terms as used by the Federal Bureau of Prisons appear in the tables:

Metropolitan Correctional Centers (MCCs)—Urban jail-type centers used for housing pre-trial detainees and sentenced offenders serving short sentences or awaiting transfer to another federal institution.

Security Level—The federal security designation system ranking institutions from 1 (least secure) to 6 (most secure). Camps and minimum security institutions are rated 1. Levels 2, 3, and 4 designate medium security institutions. Levels 5 and 6 designate maximum security institutions.

Administrative (A) Facility—An institution housing offenders at several or all levels of security.

Camps—Minimum security (Level 1) facilities operating at varying levels of independence.

Independent camp: An autonomous, self-contained operation.

Military camp: An independent camp located on a military base.

Satellite camp: A camp operated adjacent to a correctional facility and using at least some of the institution's resources.

While some of the exceptions noted for particular guidelines apply to specific federal institutions, the guidelines are presented in full in hopes that they will be of interest to the field as a whole and of use to administrators and managers at all levels.

Background

Determining and defending an efficient level of staffing for correctional institutions is an extremely formidable task. Few standards address the number of personnel required for a given type of institution. Present standards in the field of corrections generally express personnel needs in terms of the number of staff needed to attain ultimate goals rather than the specific personnel needed to provide, for example, 24-hour coverage. In addition, physical plants, missions, and programs of correctional facilities differ from institution to institution. Consequently, personnel needs are varied and multifaceted.

Nonetheless, the development of uniform criteria for equitable distribution of resources is viewed as necessary for the continued effective and efficient operation of the Bureau of Prisons and for the immediate and practical purpose of redistributing existing resources wherever appropriate.

Methodology

Although several methodological approaches are available for determining personnel needs, it was initially determined to utilize the expert opinion of program managers to establish a baseline for developing staffing patterns. Program managers were asked to determine how many personnel they would need to operate their program in a minimum, medium, and maximum security institution with a rated capacity of 500, and all were required to justify the number of positions proposed by citing standards, needs assessments, task force reports, and/or any other documentation that would support their positions.

To prevent overstatement of needs, the managers were instructed to take into account the limited amount of public resources available and to request only the number of staff needed to operate their programs effectively, i.e., not the ideal or optimum staff, but also not a skeleton staff. Given the general climate of cutback management, managers in some program areas were instructed to develop their guidelines at existing levels even though they could demonstrate the need for additional staff. For example, Financial Management and Maintenance program managers were instructed to hold their staffing guidelines within currently authorized and approved full-time positions.

As a means of assessing these responses, information on existing staffing patterns by program area was assembled for federal and state institutions. Comparison of the program managers' preliminary submissions indicated that the initial staffing guidelines were a reasonable approximation of existing staffing practices in federal institutions.

In addition, it was determined that the Bureau's level of staffing compared favorably with existing staffing patterns in state correctional systems: About half of the states had a higher staff-to-inmate ratio than the Bureau and about half had a lower ratio.

Following the establishment of a baseline staffing pattern for a facility with a rated capacity of 500, the staffing patterns were submitted to the Bureau's management for review and approval. After some minor revisions, the preliminary set of staffing guidelines was pilot-tested at several institutions in the Bureau's Western Region. This evaluation substantiated the basic soundness of the staffing pattern approach and revealed that staffing for most program areas met the requirements of the guidelines. Considerable deviations were found in the area of institutional security due to the special needs of each institution, e.g., manned towers and walls versus chain link fence and electronic security devices. This was expected, and evaluation and refinement of the guidelines continued.

To further evaluate the guidelines' accuracy and utility, a full-field study was conducted. All of the Bureau's chief executive officers were asked to compare their current authorized positions to the guidelines and to justify or explain any deviations. The study provided a wealth of information about staffing and staffing needs. Using the comments and information gained, the Executive Staff Personnel Sub-Committee reviewed and further refined the staffing guidelines. Several sets of guidelines were also referred to the program managers for further refinement. The guidelines for the institutional security program received an intensive full-field study and reevaluation. As a further test of validity, the Bureau's regional directors were also asked to review and comment on the guidelines. After additional refinements and reviews, the following set of guidelines was ultimately approved.

This, however, will not be the final answer. The development of staffing guidelines is a continuous adaptive-learning process. Corrections is a dynamic business and staffing guidelines must continue to adapt to the changing needs of the field.

Intent of the Staffing Guidelines

The staffing guidelines serve as a reference point from which staffing needs can be determined. Where specific need and circumstance dictate, deviations from the guidelines will be made; these deviations, however, must be fully documented and justified. Another important function of the guidelines is to conserve resources. Every effort should be made to operate within the guidelines or to operate with fewer personnel wherever possible.

Resource Allocation

Personnel resources are distributed according to both program priorities and the total amount of resources available. For example, if the total resources available Bureau-wide equal only 90 percent of the total resources required, each region can expect to receive 90 percent of their total calculated resource requirements. The percentage of resources allocated to various program areas, however, can be changed to meet priorities. If, for instance, it is a regional or national priority to upgrade the medical program, this program could be staffed at 100 percent, even though only 90 percent of needed resources are available, as long as staffing for other programs could be reduced to less than 90 percent.

Using the Staffing Guidelines

The staffing guidelines are listed in tables according to the Bureau's decision unit structure (e.g., Food Service, Medical Service, Staff Training). Each table provides specific guidance for determining the appropriate number and kinds of personnel needed to staff the decision unit and is divided into three sections:

- *Guidelines*—a listing and/or formula for determining the number and type of positions for an institutional program.
- *Exceptions*—situations in which exceptions are made to the guidelines.
- *Application*—a description of how to apply the guidelines.

Computation of Staffing Requirements

The staffing requirements are expressed in terms of a series of indexes that indicate the proper staffing requirement at a given level of workload. For example, in Financial Management the workload measure is the institution's rated capacity. The first index of this workload is a rated capacity of 200, and the required number of staff for this workload level is 11.

Staffing requirements for workloads falling between the indexes given may be determined by arithmetic interpolation. Those for workload levels falling above or below the indexes given can be determined by arithmetic extrapolation. Each process requires three steps. The following examples are based on Table 1, Food Service.

- *Interpolation—between intervals:* An institution with a rated capacity of 300 lies in the interval between the given indexes of 250 and 350.

1. Determine the difference between the rated capacity of the institution and the lower index.

$$300 - 250 = 50$$

2. Multiply the difference by the given interval rate and round to the nearest whole number.

$$50 \times .020 = 1$$

3. Add this amount to the total staffing requirements of the lower index.

$$6 + 1 = 7$$

Therefore the staffing requirement for Food Service at an institution with a rated capacity of 300 is 7.

- *Extrapolation—above intervals:* An institution with a rated capacity of 1095 is above 900, the highest given index.

1. Determine the difference between the rated capacity of the institution and the highest index.

$$1095 - 900 = 195$$

2. Multiply the difference by the given interval rate and round to the nearest whole number.

$$195 \times .004 = .78 = 1$$

3. Add this amount to the staffing requirements for the highest index.

$$11 + 1 = 12$$

- *Extrapolation—below intervals:* An institution with a rated capacity of 185 is below 250, the lowest given index.

1. Determine the difference between the rated capacity of the institution and the lowest index.

$$250 - 185 = 65$$

2. Multiply the difference by the given interval rate and round to the nearest whole number.

$$65 \times .020 = 1.3 = 1$$

3. Subtract this amount from the staffing requirements for the lowest given index.

$$6 - 1 = 5$$

Procedures for Determining Current Authorized Staffing Levels

To determine the current authorized staffing level the following categories of positions will be counted:
- All authorized full-time equivalent Salary and Expense positions.
- All Public Health Service positions.
- All Commissary non-appropriated positions.
- All vocational training positions funded by Federal Prison Industries.

TABLE 1
FOOD SERVICE

I. GUIDELINES

Positions	Institution Capacity				Satellite Camps
	250	350	650	900	
Food Service Admin.	1	1	1	1	0
Asst. Food Service Admin.	0	1	1	1	0
Dining Room Supervisor	0	1	3	4	0
Cook Foreman	3	3	3	3	2
Bakery	1	1	1	1	0
Relief	1	1	1	1	1
TOTAL	6	8	10	11	3
INTERVAL RATE		.020	.007	.004	

II. EXCEPTIONS

MCCs: Delete 3 positions due to no dining rooms.

Springfield: Add 2 positions for special medical diet preparation; add 2 positions for ward feeding.

Institutions that purchase baked goods: Delete 1 position.

Meat cutter positions: Count under farm program.

Institutions without full-scale bakeries or bakery supervisors: *Northeast:* New York, Otisville, Ray Brook. *Southeast:* Butner,* Memphis,* Miami,* Talladega.* *North Central:* Chicago. *South Central:* Big Spring, Bastrop. *Western:* San Diego, Boron, Florence, Pleasanton.

* Institutions have planned bakeries; positions will be adjusted when the bakeries become operational.

III. APPLICATION

Determine rated capacity of the institution (excluding satellite camp) and select appropriate guideline. If the institution has a satellite camp, use satellite camp column to determine number of positions for camp.

TABLE 2
MEDICAL SERVICE

I. GUIDELINES

Positions	Independent Camps 100–500	Institution Capacity					
		375	500	625	750	875	950
Physician	0	1	1	2	2	2	3
Psychiatrist	0	0	0	1	1	1	1
Dentist	1	1	1	1	1	2	2
Dental Asst.	0	0	0	0	0	1	1
HAO *	1	1	1	1	1	1	1
Asst. HAO	0	0	1	1	1	1	1
Health Records	1	1	1	1	2	2	3
Physician Asst.**	4	7	8	8	8	9	10
TOTAL	7	11	13	15	16	19	22
INTERVAL RATE		.016	.016	.008	.024	.040	.003

* Hospital Administrative Officer
** Includes Lab/X-Ray and pharmacist positions.

II. EXCEPTIONS

Special studies to be conducted to determine the medical staffing requirements at Fort Worth, Springfield, Butner, Lexington, Terminal Island, Eglin, Montgomery, and Marion.

New York MCC medical needs: Determined by court decision.

III. APPLICATION

Determine rated capacity of the institution and select appropriate guideline. If the institution has a satellite camp, use the combined rated capacity of the institution and the satellite camp.

TABLE 3
INSTITUTIONAL SECURITY

I. GUIDELINES

Positions	Institution Security Levels		3/ Admin[a]	4	5	6	Indepen- dent Camps	Satellite Camps[b]
	1	2						
Chief Corr. Supv.	1	1	1	1	1	1	1	
CCS[*] Clerk	1	1	1	1	2	2	1	
Corr. Supv.	7	7	7	8	9	10	4	
Security Officer	1	1	1	1	1	1	0	
Spec. Invest. Supv.	0	0	1	1	1	1	0	
Front Entrance	2.8	1.4	1.4	2.8	2.8	2.8	0	
Control Center	4.2	4.2	4.2	5.6	5.6	5.6	4.2	
Rear Entrance	1	1	1	1	2	2	0	
Inside Patrol	4.2	4.2	4.2	4.2	4.2	4.2	4.2	
Corridor Officer	4.2	4.2	4.2	4.2	7	7	0	
Unit Officers[c]								
Activities Officers[d]								
Segregation Officers[e]								
Visiting Room[f]								
Perimeter Security[g]								
Tool Control	0	0	1	1	1	1	0	
Industry Control	0	0	0	1	1	1	0	
Subtotals								
Loans to Other Serv.[h]								
Sick & Ann. Rlf.[i]								
Training Rlf.[j]								

[*] Chief Correctional Supervisor

[a] Use 2.8 officers for front entrance in Administrative facilities.

[b] Use minimum of 5.2 officers for up to 100 rated capacity. Add 4.2 officers for each additional increment of rated capacity greater than 40 but not more than 100.

[c] Use 4.2 officers per unit. A unit is considered the entire housing area that can be supervised without breaking building security.

[d] Use 1 officer per 200 rated capacity for Levels 1-2-3; 1.5 officers per 200 rated capacity for Level 4; 2 officers per 200 rated capacity for Levels 5-6; 4 officers per 200 rated capacity for Level 6. Multiply the result rounded to a whole number by 1.4 for a seven-day shift.

[e] Base guideline is a total of 5 officers (2 officers each day and evening shift plus 1 morning shift officer). If 10% of institution's rated capacity is over 30 inmates, add 1 officer for each additional 20 inmates. (Drop if overage is under 10; add if over 10.) Multiply the rounded result by 1.4 for a seven-day shift.

[f] Use minimum of 2 officers up to 400 rated capacity. Add 1 officer for each additional 400 rated capacity. (Drop if under 200, add if over 200.) Based on five-day visiting. Multiply the rounded result by 1.4 for seven-day visiting.

[g] Multiply the number of required perimeter posts (towers and patrol) by the appropriate amounts:

> Number of 1-day posts x .02
> Number of 5-day posts x 1.0
> Number of 7-day posts x 1.4

[h] 3% of subtotal on work sheet.

[i] Use 28 days per officer per year.

[j] Use 12 days per officer per year. NOTE: 1 position = 220 workdays per year.

II. EXCEPTIONS

> Bus operations: Add 3 positions.
> Airlift operations: Add 2 positions.

III. APPLICATION

Determine security level, type, and rated capacity of institution. Evaluate each position against need and determine number of positions required. Where there is no corresponding position, no position will be authorized, e.g., if the institution has no corridor officer, then no positions will be allowed for this post. Calculate loans to other service, training relief, sick relief, and annual leave relief according to *Custodial Manual* procedures. Sum total positions required.

TABLE 4
UNIT MANAGEMENT

I. GUIDELINES

Positions	General Unit Capacity		Specialized Unit Capacity	
	100	200	75	150
Unit Manager	1	1	1	1
Case Manager	1	2	1	2
Corr. Counselor	2	3	2	3
Secretary	1	1	1	1
TOTAL	5	7	5	7
INTERVAL RATE	.020		.027	

Positions	Number of Institutions 1
Case Management Coordinator	1
TOTAL	1

II. EXCEPTIONS

Butner: Add 2 positions to the psychiatric unit.

III. APPLICATION

Determine number, type, and rated capacity of each unit and select appropriate staffing level.

Each institution will also receive 1 case management coordinator.

For the purpose of guideline comparisons, psychologists in the Unit Management decision unit who do not function as unit or case managers will be counted in the Psychology decision unit.

TABLE 5
EDUCATION

I. GUIDELINES

Positions	Independent Camps & MCCs	Level 1, 5, & 6 Institutions	Level A, 2, 3, & 4 Institutions
Administrative	1	3	3
ABE	1	1	1
GED	1	1	1
College Coordinator	0	1	1
Voc. Training	0	2	4
Related Trades	0	1	2
Social Education	0	1	1
Unit/Team/Relief	0	1	1
TOTAL	3	11	14

II. EXCEPTIONS

Add 1 administrative staff position if camp capacity exceeds 300.

Only 2 vocational training and 1 related trade teachers are allowed at Springfield and level A, 2, 3, and 4 institutions with less than 400 rated capacity.

Add 1 Unit/Team/Relief position for an institution with 7 or more units.

Add 1 position for satellite camps.

III. APPLICATION

Determine security level or type of institution and select appropriate guideline.

TABLE 6
LEISURE

I. GUIDELINES

Positions	Institution Capacity				
	200	400	600	800	1000
Recreation Specialist	1	2	3	4	5
TOTAL	1	2	3	4	5
INTERVAL RATE	.005	.005	.005	.005	

II. EXCEPTIONS

MCCs: Delete 1 leisure program position regardless of capacity.
Independent camps: Minimum of 2 leisure program positions.
Satellite camps: Minimum of 1 leisure program position.

III. APPLICATION

Determine rated capacity of institution and select appropriate guideline. If there is a satellite camp, determine the rated capacity of the camp and select the appropriate standard (minimum of 1 position).

TABLE 7
RELIGION

I. GUIDELINES

Positions	Institution Capacity	
	500	1000
Staff Chaplain	1	1
Assistant	—	1
TOTAL	1	2
INTERVAL RATE	.002	

II. EXCEPTIONS

Minimum of one chaplain per institution regardless of capacity. Assistant need not be chaplain.

III. APPLICATION

Determine rated capacity of institution and select appropriate guideline. If there is a satellite camp, include rated capacity of the camp with the institution's rated capacity.

TABLE 8
PSYCHOLOGY

I. GUIDELINES

Positions	Number of General Units 2	Number of General Units 4	Number of Specialized Units 1	Number of Specialized Units 2
Psychologist*	1	2	1	2
TOTAL	1	2	1	2
INTERVAL RATE	.500		1.000	

* In addition to other assigned duties, one psychologist at each institution will be designated as chief psychologist.

II. EXCEPTIONS

Non-unitized institutions: Provide 1 psychologist for every 225 inmates.

Lexington, Springfield, Butner, and Terminal Island: Require special studies due to their special mental health programs.

Regional psychology administrators based in institutions: Count as half-time position in staffing guidelines.

III. APPLICATION

Determine number and type of units and select appropriate guideline.

For the purpose of guideline comparisons, psychologists in the Unit Management decision unit who do not function as unit or case managers will be counted in the Psychology decision unit.

TABLE 9
EXECUTIVE OFFICE

I. GUIDELINES

Positions	Institution Capacity 300–750	Institution Capacity 750 & above
Warden	1	1
Secretary	1	1
Executive Assistant*	1	1
Paralegal*	1	1
Assistant Warden	2	2
Research*	1	1
Secretary	1	2
TOTAL	8	9

Positions	Independent Camps & Satellite Camps 100–300	Independent Camps & Satellite Camps 300–500
Superintendent	1	1
Assistant	0	1
Secretary	1	1
TOTAL	2	3

II. EXCEPTIONS

Petersburg satellite camp: No executive office staff because of small size of camp.

* Executive Assistant, paralegal, and research positions: Include these positions only where they presently exist. These positions will be counted in the Executive Office cost center for the purposes of guideline comparisons.

Three associate wardens: Leavenworth and Springfield only.

III. APPLICATION

Determine type and rated capacity of institution and select appropriate guideline.

TABLE 10
FINANCIAL MANAGEMENT

I. GUIDELINES

Positions	Institution Capacity					
	200	400	600	800	900	1100 & Over
Controller	1	1	1	1	1	1
Budget & Accounting Officer	1	1	1	1	1	1
Budget Analyst	0	1	1	1	1	1
Supv. Accountant	1	1	1	1	1	1
Operating Accountant	0	0	0	1	1	1
Accounting Technician	2	2	2	2	2	2
Property Management & Procurement Officer	1	1	1	1	1	1
Property Management Officer	1	1	1	1	1	1
Contracting Officer	0	1	1	1	1	1
Procurement Officer	0	0	0	0	1	1
Supv. Warehouse Foreman	1	1	1	1	1	1
Asst. Warehouse Foreman	1	1	1	1	1	2
Warehouseman	1	1	2	3	3	3
Laundry Plant Supervisor	1	1	1	1	1	1
Asst. Laundry Plant Supv.	0	1	1	1	1	1
Laundry Plant Manager	0	0	0	0	1	2
TOTAL	11	14	15	17	19	21
INTERVAL RATE	.015	.005	.010	.020	.010	

II. EXCEPTIONS

Independent Camps: Delete 2 positions because of low staffing levels.

MCCs: Delete 2 positions because of the compactness of operation except for New York where only 1 position will be deleted because of uniqueness of operation.

Pleasanton, Seagoville, Lewisburg, Atlanta, and Leavenworth regional accounting centers: Add 1 position.

Allenwood: Delete 1 warehouse position because of small operation.

III. APPLICATION

Determine rated capacity of institution and select appropriate guideline. Include rated capacity of satellite camp in determination of total institutional capacity.

TABLE 11
PERSONNEL

I. GUIDELINES

Positions	Institution Personnel		
	100	200	350
Personnel Officer	1	1	1
Personnel Specialist	1	1	2
Personnel Clerk	0	1	1
TOTAL	2	3	4
INTERVAL RATE		.010	.007

II. EXCEPTIONS

None

III. APPLICATION

Determine total number of positions required under the staffing guidelines for all programs except personnel, plus the total number of Federal Prison Industries positions currently assigned to the institution, and then select appropriate guideline for Personnel unit.

TABLE 12
ADMINISTRATIVE SYSTEMS

I. GUIDELINES

	Institution Capacity		
Positions	200	450	750
Admin. Systems Manager	1	1	1
Admin. Systems Supervisor	1	1	1
Admin. Systems Technician	4	5	6
TOTAL	6	7	8
INTERVAL RATE		.004	.003

II. EXCEPTIONS

Satellite camp: Add 1 position.
MCCs: Add 6 positions.
Detention operations: Add 1 position.
Independent camps: Subtract 2 positions.
Bus operation: Add 1 position.
Airlift operation: Add 1 position.

III. APPLICATION

Determine rated capacity of institution and select appropriate guideline. Include rated capacity of satellite camp in determination of total institutional capacity.

TABLE 13
SAFETY

I. GUIDELINES

	Institution Capacity		
Positions	190	525	925
Safety Manager	1	1	1
Safety Clerk	—	1	1
Asst. Safety Manager	—	—	1
TOTAL	1	2	3
INTERVAL RATE		.003	.003

II. EXCEPTIONS

MCCs will be limited to 1 safety position.
All institutions will be limited to 3 positions.

III. APPLICATION

Determine rated capacity of institution and select appropriate guideline. Include rated capacity of satellite camp in determination of total institutional capacity.

TABLE 14
STAFF TRAINING

I. GUIDELINES

Positions	Number of Institutions 1
Training Coordinator	1
TOTAL	1

II. EXCEPTIONS

None

III. APPLICATION

Each institution and each independent camp will have one training coordinator.

TABLE 15
MAINTENANCE

I. GUIDELINES

Positions	Institution Security Levels 1–2	3	Admin/ 4	5	6	MCC	Ind. Camp	Mil. Camp
Base Staff*	11	12	13	14	15	10	4	3
If Motor Pool	+1	+1	+1	+1	+1	—	+1	—
If Power Plant	+7	+7	+7	+7	+7	+6	+5	—
If Sewage Plant	+1	+1	+1	+1	+1	—	—	—

*For specific positions, see staffing list following the Application section.

Size Factor: Apply the following size factors to all institutions except independent camps, military camps, and MCCs. For satellite camps, include camp's square footage in institution's square footage.

Sq. Footage in Thousands Positions		Sq. Footage in Thousands Positions	
0 - 50	− 4	700 - 750	8
50 - 100	− 3	750 - 800	9
100 - 150	− 2	800 - 850	10
150 - 200	− 1	850 - 900	11
200 - 350	—	900 - 950	12
350 - 400	+ 1	950 - 1000	13
400 - 450	2	1000 - 1050	14
450 - 500	3	1050 - 1100	15
500 - 550	4	1100 - 1150	16
550 - 600	5	1150 - 1200	17
600 - 650	6	1200 - 1250	18
650 - 700	7		

II. EXCEPTIONS

Institutions built before 1940: Add 2 positions.
Satellite camp: Add 1 position (General Mechanic).
El Reno: Add 1 position because of large number of buildings.
Seagoville and Allenwood: Consider as Level 1 institutions.
Florence: Consider as a camp but reduce to 1 position because of size.
Big Spring: Add 3 positions because of size.

III. APPLICATION

Determine type and total square footage (including satellite camp) of institution and select appropriate guideline.

Maintenance staff required to meet guidelines: *Base Staff* (11 positions. For increases above this base, add General Mechanics): Facility Manager, Clerk, General Foreman, Painter, Plumber, Carpenter, Electrician, Electronics Technician, Landscaper/Gardener, Machine and Welding, Refrigeration and Air Conditioning. *Power Plant* (7 positions): Chief Engineer, Operating Engineers (5), Steamfitter. *Motor Pool* (1 position): Garage Mechanic. *Sewage Plant* (1 position): Plant Operator. *Satellite Camp* (1 position): General Mechanic.

Copies of the Federal Bureau of Prisons' Staffing Guidelines can be obtained from: Federal Bureau of Prisons, Division of Planning and Development, 320 First St., N.W., Washington, D.C. 20534.

Planners and designers of new or remodeled facilities should consider *all* ACA Standards and their relationship to space allocation and design criteria. However, the following standards are especially critical in facility planning and are presented as important reminders which should be reviewed frequently during the design process of adult correctional facilities.

Administration, Organization and Management

2-4022 The institution provides for all inmates the following constructive programs, including, at a minimum: reception and orientation; evaluation and classification; academic education equivalent to high school; vocational training; employment; religious services; social services and counseling; psychological and psychiatric services; library services; medical and dental health care; athletic, recreational and leisure time activities; inmate involvement with community groups; mail and visiting; access to media, legal materials, attorneys and courts; volunteer services; and prerelease orientation and planning.

2-4033 At least annually, the warden/superintendent reviews space requirements and the need for capital improvements; requests for needed budget allocations are recorded in writing.

2-4049 There is an inmate commissary or canteen where inmates can purchase items not furnished by the facility from an approved list. Strict controls are maintained over its operation and standard accounting procedures are followed.

2-4083 The institution's training and staff development plan provides for an ongoing formal evaluation of all pre-service, in-service, and specialized training programs, with a written report prepared annually.

2-4084 Library and reference services are available to complement the training and staff development program.

2-4086 Space and equipment required for the training and staff development program is available.

2-4116 The institution maintains a cumulative case history on each inmate in a master file that includes, but is not limited to these items: important events; significant decisions and their rationale for the decisions; dates on which services were rendered; and inmate institutional adjustment. This master file is placed in a secure location.

2-4127 Existing, renovation, addition. Institutions of more than 500 inmates are subdivided into units of not more than 500 inmates each which are staffed by a unit manager and the number and variety of personnel required to provide the program services and custodial supervision needed for each unit.

DISCUSSION: Units of 500 or less inmates permit programs to be conducted on a smaller, more manageable scale and decisions affecting inmates to be made by those personnel who know them best. Such units should be semi-autonomous as related to matters within the unit, counseling services and intra-institution classification, and custodial supervision. (See related standard 2-4160)

2-4128 Existing, renovation, addition, new plant. The population assigned to housing units does not exceed the rated bed capacity of the facility.

2-4129 Existing, renovation, addition, new plant. Only one inmate occupies a room or cell designed for single occupancy which has a floor area of at least 60 square feet, provided inmates spend no more than 10 hours per day locked in. When confinement exceeds 10 hours per day, there are at least 80 square feet of floor space.

2-4130 Existing, renovation, addition, new plant. Each room or cell has, at a minimum, the following facilities and conditions:
Sanitation facilities, including access to:
- Toilet above floor level which is available for use without staff assistance 24 hours a day; and
- Wash basin with hot and cold running water

A bed at above floor level, desk, hooks or closet space, chair or stool
Natural light
Documentation by an independent, qualified source that:
- Lighting is at least 20 footcandles at desk level and in the personal grooming area;
- Circulation is at least 10 cubic feet of outside or recirculated filtered air per minute per human occupant;
- Temperatures are appropriate to the summer and winter comfort zones; and noise levels do not exceed 70 decibels in daytime and 45 decibels at night.

DISCUSSION: Sensory deprivation should be reduced by providing variety in terms of space, surface textures and colors. Natural lighting should be available either by cell or room windows to exterior or from a source within 20 feet of the room or cell. The bed should be elevated from the floor and have a clean, covered mattress with blankets provided as needed. Suggested temperatures are 66 to 80 degrees Fahrenheit in the summer comfort zone, optimally 71 degrees, and 61 to 73 degrees Fahrenheit in the winter comfort zone, optimally 70 degrees.

2-4131 Existing, renovation, addition, new plant (minimum security only). Where used, multiple occupancy rooms house no less than three and no more than 50 inmates each who are screened for suitability to group living prior to admission. Multiple occupancy rooms are continuously observed by staff and provide the following facilities and conditions:

A minimum floor area of 50 square feet per occupant in the sleeping area and a clear floor to ceiling height of not less than eight feet;

Toilet and shower facilities at a minimum of one operable toilet and shower for every eight occupants;

One operable wash basin with hot and cold running water for every six occupants;

Single beds only;

Access to a locker or private storage space for each occupant;

Natural light;

Documentation by an independent, qualified source that lighting is at least 20 footcandles at desk level and in the personal grooming area;

Circulation is at least 10 cubic feet of outside or recirculated filtered air per minute per occupant;

Temperatures are appropriate to the summer and winter comfort zones; and noise levels that do not exceed 70 decibels in daytime and 45 decibels at night.

DISCUSSION: Where multiple occupancy housing cannot be avoided, as in dormitories, or where it is used in minimum security conditions as a preferred living situation, the number of inmates rooming together should be kept as low as possible. All inmates placed in multiple occupancy housing should be carefully screened by the classification committee or other authorized group prior to assignment. Chairs and tables should be provided either in the sleeping area or dayroom for reading and writing. (See related standards 2-4152, 2-4401, and 2-4405)

2-4132 Existing, renovation, addition, new plant. Minimum security institutions, or minimum security areas within larger institutions provide individual rooms with key control shared by the occupants and staff, or continuous access to toilet and shower facilities and hot and cold running water, including drinking water. Rooms also provide the following facilities and conditions:
A minimum floor area of 60 square feet;
A bunk at above floor level, desk, hooks or closet space, chair or stool;
Natural light;
Documentation by an independent, qualified source that:
- Lighting is at least 20 footcandles at desk level and in the personal grooming area;
- Circulation is at least 10 cubic feet of outside or recirculated filtered air per minute per occupant;
- Temperatures are appropriate to the summer and winter comfort zones; and noise levels do not exceed 70 decibels in daytime and 45 decibels at night.

2-4133 Existing, renovation, addition, new plant. When males and females are housed in the same institution there are separate sleeping quarters.

2-4134 Existing, renovation, addition, new plant. There are two identifiable exits in each inmate housing area and other high density areas to permit the prompt evacuation of inmates and staff under emergency conditions. (Mandatory)

2-4135 Existing, renovation, addition, new plant. The segregation housing units provide living conditions that approximate those of the general inmate population; all exceptions are clearly documented. Segregation housing units provide the following facilities and conditions:
Single occupancy rooms or cells with a floor area of at least 80 square feet;
Sanitation facilities, including access to:
- Above-floor toilet facilities available for use without staff assistance 24 hours per day;
- Hot and cold running water.
Natural light;
A bunk at above floor level, desk or writing space and stool;
Documentation by an independent, qualified source that:
- Lighting is at least 20 footcandles at desk level and in the personal grooming area;
- Circulation is at least 10 cubic feet of fresh or purified air per minute;
- Temperatures are appropriate to the summer and winter comfort zones; and noise levels do not exceed 70 decibels in daytime and 45 decibels at night.

2-4136 Existing, renovation, addition, new plant. The segregation rooms permit inmates assigned to them to converse with others in the same housing unit and have doors which permit observation by staff.

2-4137 Existing, renovation. There is a separate day room leisure time space for each general population housing unit.

2-4138 Existing, renovation. Space outside the cell or room is provided for inmate exercise.

2-4139 Existing, renovation, addition, new plant. In institutions offering academic and vocational training programs, the classrooms are designed in cooperation with school authorities.

2-4140 Existing, renovation, addition, new plant. There is a visiting room or area for contact visiting and, if necessary, a visiting area for non-contact visiting, both of which provide a reasonable degree of privacy.
DISCUSSION: While security must be observed, some degree of privacy can enhance the value of visits for both the inmate and the visitor. There should be separate restrooms for inmates and visitors, both male and female. There should be adequately designed space to permit screening and searching of both inmates and visitors. Space should be provided for the proper storage of visitors' coats, handbags, and other possessions not allowed into the visiting area.

2-4141 Existing, renovation, addition, new plant. Space is provided for an inmate commissary or canteen, or provisions are made for a mobile commissary service.
DISCUSSION: An area should be provided near inmate housing quarters where inmates can purchase personal items. The size of the canteen should be commensurate with the size of the inmate population. When security considerations dictate, staff members may take movable carts to cell blocks instead.

2-4142 Existing, renovation, addition, new plant. If the institution has watchtowers, they are placed so that they permit an unobstructed view of the grounds and perimeter and are equipped with the weaponry, lighting, sighting, and communications devices necessary for effective execution of their function.

2-4143 Existing, renovation, addition, new plant. The food preparation and dining area includes a space for food preparation based on population size.

2-4144 Existing, renovation, addition, new plant. Space is provided for administrative, custodial, professional and clerical staff; this space includes conference rooms, employee lounge, storage room for records, public lobby and toilet facilities.

2-4145 Existing, renovation, addition, new plant. Handicapped inmates are housed in a manner which provides for their safety and security. Cells or housing units used by them are designed for their use, and provide the maximum possible integration with the general population. Appropriate institution programs and activities are accessible to handicapped inmates confined in the facility.
DISCUSSION: Severely handicapped inmates may be housed in special facilities. When the institution accepts handicapped individuals, provisions must be made for their housing and for their use of facility resources.

2-4146 Existing, renovation, addition, new plants. All parts of the facility which are accessible to the public are accessible to and usable by handicapped staff and visitors.

2-4147 Existing, renovation, addition, new plant. Space is provided for janitor closets, which are equipped with a sink and cleaning implements.

2-4148 Existing, renovation, addition, new plant. There are storage rooms in the institution for clothing, bedding, and cleaning supplies.

2-4149 Existing, renovation, addition, new plant. There is storage space available for the personal property of inmates.

2-4150 Existing, renovation, addition, new plant. Separate and adequate space is provided for mechanical equipment.

DISCUSSION: Sufficient space should be provided for equipment needed for heating, ventilating, air conditioning, water supply, waste removal, electricity, communications, etc. In smaller facilities, space for this equipment should constitute no more than 12 percent of all floor space. In facilities of up to 100,000 square feet, about eight percent of all floor space should be allocated for this equipment.

2-4152 Renovation, addition, new plant. Planning precludes the use of dormitories for inmate housing in maximum, close, or medium security institutions.

2-4153 Renovation, addition, new plant. The institution conforms to applicable federal, state, and local building codes.

DISCUSSION: Often a state or local jurisdiction will license an institution; this licensing indicates compliance with all building codes. In those cases in which a license is not issued, letters or certificates of compliance are acceptable. In the event the agency is not subject to local building codes, appropriate state or national codes will be applied to the institution.

2-4154 Renovation, addition, new plant. There is documentation by an independent, qualified source that ventilation is at least 10 cubic feet of outside or recirculated filtered air per minute, per human occupant, for cell blocks and guard stations, and 20 cubic feet per minute for eating halls. Lighting requirements for the facility are determined by the tasks to be performed, interior surface finishes and colors, type and spacing of light sources, outside lighting, and shadows and glare.

2-4155 Renovation, addition, new plant. There is documentation by a qualified source that the interior finishing material in inmate living areas, exit areas, and places of public assembly are in accordance with recognized national fire safety codes. (Mandatory)

DISCUSSION: No institutional furnishings, ceilings, partitions, or floors should be constructed of foamed plastics or foamed rubber unless the fire performance characterisitcs of the material are known and acceptable. (See related standard 2-4166)

2-4156 Renovation, addition, new plant. There is a separate indoor space for vigorous exercise in inclement weather; this space is no less than 60 x 100 feet with a ceiling height of no less than 22 feet.

2-4157 Renovation, addition, new plant. There is a minimum of two acres of outdoor recreation space for each inmate unit of up to 500 inmates; additional outdoor recreation space is provided at the rate of 90 square feet per inmate over 500.

DISCUSSION: Recreation opportunities provide healthful, relaxing activities for inmates, and create outlets for reducing tension. Recreation areas should contain space and equipment for track, weight lifting, baseball, handball activities, etc., to provide for a variety of interests.

(See related standard 2-4458)

2-4158 Addition, new plant. There is separate dayroom/leisure time space for each general population housing unit containing 35 square feet of floor space per inmate exclusive of circulation corridors in front of cells/rooms.

DISCUSSION: Dayrooms should have enough floor space to allow for a variety of activities, such as reading, writing, table games, and television. Circulation corridors in front of cells/rooms should not be included in computing dayroom area. (See related standard 2-4137)

2-4159 Addition, new plant. Administrative segregation housing units are the same as those for the general population and have an area for indoor exercise outside the room or cell that has 35 square feet of floor space per inmate requiring exercise.

2-4160 New plants. The institution is designed to accommodate no more than 500 inmates.

2-4161 New plants. The institution is located within 50 miles of a civilian population center of at least 10,000 people, or minimally within one hour driving time of a hospital, fire protection, and public transportation.

2-4162 There is documentation by an independent, qualified source that the institution complies with the applicable fire safety code(s). (Mandatory)

DISCUSSION: Local or state fire codes must be strictly adhered to in order to ensure the safety and well-being of the inmates and staff. Reports of periodic inspections and action with respect to such reports must be available. In the event local and/or state codes are not applicable, the requirements of the National Fire Protection Association Life Safety Code, (current edition) apply. (See related standards 2-4164 and 2-4172)

2-4165 The institution has an automatic fire alarm and smoke detection system which is certified by an independent, qualified inspector trained in the application of national fire safety codes. If the institution depends on a local fire department, the fire alarm system is connected directly to the local fire department. Whenever possible, all system elements are tested on a quarterly basis; adequacy and operation of the systems are certified by a state fire official or other qualified authority annually. (Mandatory)

2-4166 Specifications for the selection and purchase of facility furnishings indicate the fire safety performance requirements of the materials selected. (Mandatory)

DISCUSSION: Furnishings, mattresses, cushions, or other items of foamed plastics or foamed rubber (i.e., polyurethane, polystyrene) may pose a severe hazard due to high smoke production, rapid burning once ignited, and high heat release. Such materials should be subjected to careful fire safety evaluation before purchase or use. It is recommended that cotton mattresses treated with boric acid be used. All polyurethane mattresses should be removed. (See related standard 2-4155)

2-4167 Institution facilities are equipped with noncombustible receptacles for smoking materials and separate containers for other combustible refuse at accessible locations throughout living quarters in the institution. Special containers are provided for flammable liquids and for rags used with flammable liquids. All receptacles and containers are emptied and cleaned daily. (Mandatory)

DISCUSSION: The proper and safe containment of flammable materials and the sanitation of such containers are essential activities in fire prevention.

2-4168 The facility has exits which are distinctly and permanently marked, continuously visible at all times, kept clear, and maintained in usable condition. (Mandatory)

DISCUSSION: No battery-operated electric light, portable lamp or lantern should be used for primary illumination of exits, but electric battery-operated lighting may be used as an emergency source where normal lighting has failed, as defined in the NFPA National Electrical Code. These requirements also apply to exits in buildings of public or common use.

2-4169 An independent, qualified inspector who is trained in the application of national fire safety codes has certified that the travel distance to all exits is in compliance with code requirements. (Mandatory)

DISCUSSION: When no other national code applies, the Life Safety Code specifies the travel distances from various points in the institution for areas with and without sprinkler systems. (See related standard 2-4134)

2-4170 The institution has equipment necessary to maintain essential lights, power and communications in an emergency.

DISCUSSION: The institution should have emergency power units, either battery or motor driven, to provide essential lighting and to maintain the life-sustaining functions within the institution and to continue communications with outside interests. (See related standard 2-4213)

2-4173 Written policy and procedure specify the means for the immediate release of inmates from locked areas in case of emergency, and provide for a back-up system.

DISCUSSION: The responsibilities of personnel in an emergency situation should be clearly defined. They should be aware of the location and identification of keys and be knowledgeable about all evacuation routes. Inmates should receive instructions concerning emergency procedures. A control station or other locations which are removed from the inmate living area are provided with reliable, manual means for releasing locks on swinging and sliding doors to permit prompt release of inmates in the event of fire or other emergency.

2-4175 Written policy and procedure govern the control and use of all flammable, toxic and caustic materials. (Mandatory)

DISCUSSION: Items such as lye, insecticide, antifreeze and denatured alcohol can cause death or serious injury. Provisions should be made to ensure that inmates are never in possession of such items unless they are under constant supervision by qualified personnel. Such materials should be stored in secure areas that are inaccessible to inmates, and a prescribed system should be used to account for their distribution.

2-4177 The institution's perimeter is controlled by an appropriate means to provide that inmates remain within the perimeter and to prevent access by the general public without the appropriate authorization.

DISCUSSION: Maximum (or close) and medium security institutions usually require walls or fences, with buffer zones between the buildings and recreation grounds and the barrier. If two fences are used, they should be at least 10 feet apart, and one should be imbedded in concrete for its entire length. Most minimum security institutions rely on single fences, or no fences at all, using various combinations of mechanical surveillance devices (electronic, pressure, sound or laser systems) and mobile patrols to ensure a safe perimeter.

2-4179 Safety vestibules and sally ports constitute the only breaches in the institution perimeter security. (Essential—maximum and medium security facilities only)

2-4180 Pedestrian and vehicular traffic should enter and leave at designated points in the perimeter. (Essential—medium and minimum security facilities only)

2-4181 The institution maintains a control center to provide order and security.

2-4187 The institution has facilities for the safe unloading and reloading of firearms.

2-4189 Firearms, chemical agents and related security equipment are stored in a secure but readily accessible depository outside inmate housing and activity areas, and are inventoried at least monthly to determine their condition and expiration dates.

DISCUSSION: The institution should maintain an arsenal for the secure storage and maintenance of all its firearms, ammunition, chemical agents, and other security devices. The arsenal should be located outside the inmate housing and activities area. Written policy should specify who has access to the arsenal.

2-4197 Written policy and procedure govern the control and use of tools, culinary and medical equipment.

DISCUSSION: Tools and utensils such as hacksaws, welding equipment, butcher knives and barber shears can cause death or serious injury. They should be locked in control panels and issued in accordance with a prescribed system. Provisions should be made for checking tools and utensils in and out, and for the control of their use at all times.

2-4224 Written policy and procedure provide that inmates in segregation have the opportunity to shave and shower at least three times per week.

2-4227 Written policy and procedure provide that inmates in segregation are provided opportunities for visitation, unless there are substantial reasons for withholding such privileges.

2-4228 Written policy and procedure provide that inmates in disciplinary detention are allowed limited telephone privileges, except for calls related specifically to access to the attorney of record, unless authorized by the warden/superintendent or designee.

2-4229 Written policy and procedure provide that inmates in administrative segregation and protective custody are allowed telephone privileges.

2-4232 Written policy and procedure provide that inmates in segregation receive a minimum of one hour per day, five days per week, of exercise outside their cells, unless security or safety considerations dictate otherwise.

2-4241 Written policy and procedure provide for special diets as prescribed by appropriate medical or dental personnel. (Mandatory)

DISCUSSION: Therapeutic diets should be available upon medical authorization. Specific diets should be prepared and served to inmates according to the orders of the treating physician or dentist, or as directed by the responsible health authority official. Medical diet prescriptions should be specific and complete, furnished in writing to the food service manager, and rewritten monthly. Special diets should be kept as simple as possible and should conform as closely as possible to the foods served other inmates.

2-4242 Written policy and procedure provide for special diets for inmates whose religious beliefs require the adherence to religious dietary laws.

2-4245 Toilet and wash basin facilities are available to food service personnel and inmates in the vicinity of the food preparation area.

2-4247 There are sanitary, temperature-controlled storage facilities for the storage of all foods.

2-4250 Space is provided for group dining except when security or safety considerations justify otherwise.

2-4256 The institution's potable water source and supply, whether owned and operated by the public water department or the institution, is certified by an independent, outside source to be in compliance with jurisdictional laws and regulations. (Mandatory)

2-4259 The institution provides for waste disposal. (Mandatory)

2-4265 The store of clothing, linen, and bedding exceeds that required for the facility's inmate population.

2-4266 The institution provides for the thorough cleaning and, when necessary, disinfecting of inmate personal clothing before storage or before allowing the inmate to keep and wear personal clothing.

2-4268 There are sufficient bathing facilities in the housing areas to permit inmates in the general population to shower at least three times per week.

2-4269 Water for showers is thermostatically controlled to ensure the safety of the inmates.

2-4270 There are hair care services available to inmates which comply with applicable health requirements.

2-4275 An adequately equipped medical facility, which meets the legal requirements for a licensed general hospital with respect to the services it offers, is available to all inmates. (Mandatory)

2-4277 Space, equipment, supplies, and materials for health services are provided and maintained as determined by the health authority.

2-4295 Written policy and procedure require that routine and emergency dental care is provided to each inmate under the direction and supervision of a dentist with appropriate state or federal licensure. The individual treatment plan includes the following:

Dental screening, unless completed within the previous six months, conducted on initial intake with instruction on hygiene;

Dental examinations within three months, supported by x-rays if necessary, based on information from intake screening;

A defined charting system which identifies the oral health condition and specifies the priorities of treatment by category;

Consultation with referral to recognized specialists in dentistry.

2-4305 Written policy and procedure make available chronic and convalescent care to inmates of the facility.

2-4306 Written policy and procedure require that gradual detoxification from alcohol, opiates, hypnotics, other stimulants, and sedative hypnotic drugs is effected as follows:

When performed at the facility, it is under medical supervision; and

When not performed in the facility, arrangements are made for it to be conducted in a hospital or community detoxification center.

2-4317 Written policy and procedure provide for the proper management of pharmaceuticals, and addresses the following subjects:

A formulary specifically developed for the facility;

Prescription practices which require that:

- Psychotropic medications are prescribed only when clinically indicated as one facet of a program of therapy;
- "Stop order" time periods are required for all medications;
- The prescribing provider reevaluates a prescription prior to its renewal.

Procedures for medication receipt, storage, dispensing and administration or distribution;

Maximum security storage and periodic inventory of all controlled substances, syringes and needles;

Dispensing of medicine in conformance with appropriate federal and state law;

Administration of medication which is carried out by persons properly trained and under the supervision of the health authority and facility administrator or designee;

Accountability for administering or distributing medications in a timely manner, according to physician orders.

(Mandatory)

2-4325 Written policy and procedure exist to assist inmates in making confidential contact with attorneys and their authorized representatives.

2-4326 Written policy and procedure provide for the right of inmates to have access to an appropriate law library and to supplies and services related to legal matters. The law library includes, at a minimum, relevant and up-to-date constitutional, statutory and case law materials, applicable court rules, and practice treatises. When an inmate is unable to make meaningful use of the law library alone, additional assistance necessary for effective access is provided.

2-4336 Written policy and procedure grant inmates the right to practice their religion, subject only to the limitations necessary to maintain institutional order and security.

2-4337 Written policy and procedure grant inmates the right to receive visits, subject only to the limitations necessary to maintain institutional order and security.

2-4379 Written policy and procedure provide for inmate access to public telephones.

2-4382 Written policy and procedure specify visitor registration upon entry into the institution and the circumstances under which visitors may be searched.

2-4383 Written policy and procedure provide that inmate visiting facilities permit informal communication, including opportunity for physical contact. Devices that preclude physical contact are not used except in instances of substantiated security risk.

2-4385   Written policy and procedure govern special visits.

2-4388   Written policy and procedure govern the reception and orientation of new inmates and are reviewed annually and updated if necessary.

2-4389   Written procedures for admission of inmates new to the system include, but are not limited to, the following:

Determination that the individual is legally committed to the institution;

Complete search of the individual and possessions;

Disposition of personal property;

Shower and hair care, if necessary;

Issue of clean, laundered clothing as needed;

Photographing and fingerprinting, including notation of identifying marks or other unusual physical characteristics;

Medical, dental, and mental health screening;

Assignment to a housing unit;

Recording basic personal data and information to be used for mail and visiting list;

Assisting inmates in notifying their next of kin and families of admission;

Explanation of procedures for mail and visiting;

Assigning a registered number to the inmate;

Giving written orientation materials to inmate.

2-4392   Written policy and procedure specify the personal property inmates can retain in their possession.

2-4416   Policy and procedure provide that all institutional work, industrial, and vocational/educational programs meet minimum federal, state and local work, health, and safety standards; there is documentation of at least annual health and safety inspections by federal, state, and/or local officials. Weekly inspection of all such programs are conducted by qualified institution staff. (Mandatory)

2-4419   Written policy and procedure establish furlough and work release programs to provide additional employment opportunities for inmates, consistent with the requirements of institutional and community security.

2-4421   The inmate work plan includes provision for employment for handicapped inmates.

2-4422   There is a comprehensive education program available to all eligible inmates that extends from literacy training through high school and includes communication skills, mathematics, and social science.

2-4431   The educational program is supported by specialized equipment, including, at a minimum, classrooms, teaching carrels, audiovisual materials and facilities, chalkboards, and administrative space.

2-4436   Postsecondary programs in academic and vocational education are available to qualified inmates.

2-4437   The institution uses community resources in developing academic and vocational education programs for selected inmates.

2-4439   Vocational training programs are integrated with academic programs and are relevant to the vocational needs of inmates and to employment opportunities in the community.

2-4440   Written policy and procedure govern the maintenance and handling of educational/vocational records.

2-4442   The institution maintains and/or provides access to comprehensive library services which include, but are not limited to, a reference collection which includes general and specialized materials, and planned and continuous acquisition of materials to meet the needs of the institutional staff and inmates.

2-4452   Written policy and procedure provide for a comprehensive recreational program that includes leisure time activities comparable with those available in the community.

2-4458   Facilities and equipment, which are maintained in good condition and are suitable for the planned leisure activities, are available in proportion to the inmate population.

2-4470   The institution provides facilities and equipment for the conduct of religious programs for inmates.

Copies of the Standards for Adult Correctional Institutions may be obtained from: American Correctional Association, 4321 Hartwick Road, Suite L-208, College Park, Maryland 20740.

**Design Guide for
Secure Adult
Correctional
Facilities**

This book was composed in Garamond text and Alberta display type by Capitol Communication Systems, Inc. from a design by Jean Mettee. It was printed on 70-lb. Patina Matte using five colors by Kingsport Press.
The pictures in this book were taken at the following facilities:
Douglas County Correctional Center, Omaha, Nebraska;
Federal Correctional Institution, Bastrop, Texas;
Federal Correctional Institution, Butner, North Carolina;
Federal Correctional Institution, Fort Worth, Texas;
Federal Correctional Institution, Memphis, Tennessee;
Federal Correctional Institution, Otisville, New York;
Federal Correctional Institution, Raybrook, New York;
Regional Correctional Facility, Mercer, Pennsylvania;
South Central Correctional Center, Eagle River, Alaska;
Washtenaw County Correctional Center, Ann Arbor, Michigan.
The authors wish to express their sincere thanks for the assistance provided by these facilities.

207

This publication is presented by the
American Correctional Association
as a result of the combined efforts
of a competent and capable
committee. We sincerely appreciate
their participation.

Gary Mote
Chairman, AIA

Donna Bergen

Allen Breed

Aaron Brown

Anthony P. Travisono
Executive Director, ACA

Vernon Housewright

Perry M. Johnson

Deborah Lemonias

H. G. 'Gus' Moeller
President, ACA

John McGough

Robert F. Messmer

Frederic D. Moyer

Hardy Rauch

Donald C. Voth

James H. Webster

William K. Wilkey

Norman Wirkler